DEMORALIZED

DEMORALIZED

Why Teachers Leave
the Profession They Love
and How They Can Stay

DORIS A. SANTORO

Harvard Education Press
Cambridge, Massachusetts

Paperback ISBN 978-1-68253-132-7
Library Edition ISBN 978-1-68253-133-4

Library of Congress Cataloging-in-Publication Data

Names: Santoro, Doris A., author.
Title: Demoralized : why teachers leave the profession they love and how they
    can stay / Doris A. Santoro.
Description: Cambridge, Massachusetts : Harvard Education Press, 2018. |
    Includes bibliographical references and index.
Identifiers: LCCN 2017046120| ISBN 9781682531327 (pbk.) | ISBN 9781682531334
    (library edition)
Subjects: LCSH: Teacher morale—United States. | Teacher turnover—United
    States. | Teachers—Job satisfaction—United States. | Teachers—Job
    stress—United States. | School environment—United States. |
    Teachers—Professional ethics—United States. | Teachers—Training
    of—United States.
Classification: LCC LB2833.2 .S34 2018 | DDC 371.1001/9—dc23
LC record available at https://lccn.loc.gov/2017046120

Published by Harvard Education Press,
an imprint of the Harvard Education Publishing Group

Harvard Education Press
8 Story Street
Cambridge, MA 02138

Figure 5.1 Design: Katharine Atwood
Cover Design: Ciano Design
Cover Image: Pobytov/Digital Vision Vectors/Getty Images

The typefaces used in this book are Adobe Garamond Pro, Helvetica Neue, and ITC Legacy Sans.

I feel I must emphasize and explain repeatedly the moral dimensions of all social life, and point out that morality is, in fact, hidden in everything. And this is true: whenever I encounter a problem in my work and try to get to the bottom of it, I always discover some moral aspect, be it apathy, unwillingness to recognize personal error or guilt, reluctance to give up certain positions and the advantages flowing from them, envy, an excess of self-assurance, or whatever.

—VÁCLEV HAVEL,
"POLITICS, MORALITY & CIVILITY"

Contents

Foreword

I have come to believe that in certain fields the "bad apple" rate is very low. Of course, "bad" physicians and "bad" teachers exist. But almost everyone who goes into these fields has a purpose that is somehow related to "doing good work." They enter each of these professions to make a difference; to help make the world a little bit better. Aspiring physicians and teachers hold, sometimes quite deeply, moral convictions about the worth of the work in which they want to engage. Thus, the "bad apple" rate in these professions is likely to be low. To find these "bad" practitioners, the medical and educational professions, along with state and federal legislators, have set up elaborate, but ultimately destructive, programs designed to find and eliminate those few harmful or incompetent professionals. Such programs often are supported by the public, glad to be protected from incompetent medical and educational personnel, but these same programs can seriously demoralize the vast majority of knowledgeable, experienced, committed, expert professionals in each of these fields. It turns out, as education professor Doris Santoro aptly argues in this important new book, when teachers cannot enact the values that motivate and sustain their work, demoralization is a common response.

In *Demoralized: Why Teachers Leave the Profession They Love and How They Can Stay*, Santoro does a terrific job, in fact, of turning the spotlight on this underreported and underappreciated phenomenon of demoralization. Distinguishing it from *burnout*, a word used to describe many forms of teacher dissatisfaction, she categorizes its common sources and, in doing so, lends legitimacy to this problem, opening the door to new ways to think about how to deal with it.

For educators, demoralization is a natural accompaniment to being told to fix the lives of children born into poverty. That is not easy to do. However, Santoro shows us that demoralization also occurs in our nation's well-funded and well-regarded public schools. Demoralization among teachers is a natural response to unfair evaluation systems that hold teachers accountable for standardized test scores influenced to a far greater extent by family and neighborhood, than by schooling. Demoralization among teachers also occurs as a function of being denigrated, sometimes vilified, by too many uninformed politicians and journalists. In particular, the voices of political leaders are heard, and teachers are required to adhere to the laws they pass. But the voices raised by experienced and admired classroom teachers, as responses to the laws that are made, are neither heard nor respected.

The international movement to intensify the work of the profession—to achieve more with less resources—is another source of demoralization among teachers, across nations. And demoralization also occurs among teachers when they have to cope with being squeezed economically in a society that may be paying too little in taxes to properly pay many of its public servants.

These and a dozen other contemporary sources of demoralization among experienced teachers described in this book are leading to their exiting from the profession in substantial numbers. Of course, when that happens, the knowledge they gained to be successful in their educational career is lost with them. This is true because reasonable estimates suggest that teachers' grow in their ability to influence student achievement for seven to ten years. Moreover, the total costs to replace an experienced teacher may be quite high, easily $15,000 in many of our nations' school districts. Furthermore, there is evidence that higher rates of teacher turnover negatively affect student achievement. So demoralization among America's teaching corps has serious educational and fiscal consequences. Santoro provides critical insights into the lives of those teachers who feel such demoralization and offers a compelling case for why their concerns are legitimate and should be taken seriously by district leaders, union leaders, and policy makers. They are not burning out—they are disturbed not to be contributing to education in the ways that they had hoped. In fact, Santoro argues that many of the teachers who leave the profession after years of successful and personally rewarding teaching may be more like conscientious objectors than they are like failing teachers. They leave teaching because they have ethical concerns about the work they are doing. They cannot practice the profession as they intended. As one teachers says: "We have been taken away from (the sources) of our reward." And as might be expected, they do not all live easily with that sadness.

Our nation seems not to know how contemporary educational policy, and the leadership of schools that carries out those policies, is demoralizing so many of our nation's teachers. The teachers who speak in this book believe that they are witnessing the loss of their profession, and they feel powerless to stem its disappearance. Santoro captures the teachers' despair; they mourn and express many of the symptoms associated with grief of a loved one.

However, after many deeply troubling stories of teachers' disillusionment over not being able to do good work, we learn that all but one of the experienced teachers in Santoro's book stay.

Thankfully, for those who persist, a way forward is found. They find a way to recommit to the dreams they held. They find ways to believe that they can still "do good" in education. Santoro analyzes their strategies and offers a framework that other teachers can use. Re-moralization, as Santoro asserts, does take place. And when that happens, teachers find ways to lead meaningful lives for themselves, and once again, help our nation, as well. Our nation is lucky to have these fine educators still working to make the world a bit better.

I found something quite interesting in the persuasive and engrossing stories recounted and analyzed in this book. It was a realization that these expressions of dissatisfaction with the teaching profession were not those of an ordinary group of complainers, as every profession has. Rather, the dissatisfaction expressed by these teachers is coming from deep commitments to the moral and ethical principles that define our remarkable system of public education. I found in the contemporary concerns of these teachers echoes of Thomas Jefferson, John Adams, and Horace Mann. These were not ordinary complainers at all! And it left me thinking that to ignore the concerns of these teachers—the concerns of such committed and exemplary professional educators—really would make us a nation at risk.

So what can readers expect from this insightful book? Readers will gain insight into the contemporary shortage of classroom teachers that we are experiencing and the role that current educational policies play in driving away experienced, talented teachers. They can expect to "hear" the authentic voices of teachers who want to do well, and who are frequently blocked from doing so. They will be privy to remarkably insightful analyses of these lamentations along with strategies for counteracting demoralization collected by one of the most astute scholars in our research community. And they will also learn about the remarkably empowering effects that reframing and distinguishing some forms of teacher dissatisfaction as demoralization, rather than burnout, can have on teachers and those who care about strengthening rather than harming the profession. School leaders and policy makers will need to reconsider the levers that they use to address teacher shortage and retention problems. They damage the profession and our schools by targeting all teachers as "bad apples" and by neglecting to take a deeper look at the sources of teacher dissatisfaction.

David C. Berliner
Regents' Professor Emeritus
Mary Lou Fulton Teachers College
Arizona State University

INTRODUCTION

I didn't disagree with the letter. It was more ... the disappointment in myself for having become a teacher I didn't like.

   —Carla, a twenty-three-year teaching veteran, in tears as she describes the letter of reprimand she was issued by her principal.

You play ball or leave with your ethics.

   —Reggie taught for ten years. He resigned in 2015.

As a teacher, my job is to answer questions for kids. As a teacher, it's my job to make my students feel safe, cared for, and part of a community. They're nine years old. They have certain adults in their lives that they're supposed to be able to trust and that they care for. The fact that [my student] felt that she was hurting me in any way, shape, or form by not being able to perform [on a test] was wrong ... I had words and actions of things that I wanted to be as a teacher, and I was able to enact them until this point. And at this point, no longer am I allowed to be that person that I know I want to be. I have to be this other person who feels monstrous, actually.

—Diane, who has taught for twenty-one years, recalls first administering a high-stakes test.

I wish Arne Duncan [former US Secretary of Education] would come to my living room. [I would tell him] I really cared about kids and I wanted to connect with them. I don't think I wasn't who [accountability proponents] wanted me to be. I think I was the teacher they would've wanted, you know. And yet they broke me . . . And so the only people that you really damaged were the people who were already invested and caring and dedicated.

—Gina, a National Board certified teacher with thirteen years of experience, was Teacher of the Year for her state. The following year she took a disability leave as a direct result of the increased workload associated with accountability measures mandated by her school.

There were always these people that were the type of teachers—the June, July, August teacher—counting the years to retirement teacher. You run into that in any field. So, I was like, alright, I'm definitely not that kind of teacher . . . I'm going until I'm blue-haired, you know, as long as I can still be funny and make it fun, I'm good. And I see more teachers who would never say ["I'm leaving teaching."], talking about retirement. In my worst moments, I say I'm never going to make it to retirement. I'm never going to have a pension . . . I wanted to make enough [money] and I wanted to be happy and love what I do. So I worry that more teachers, good teachers, who wouldn't be leaving, are leaving earlier.

—Vanessa entered teaching after a career in marketing and has been teaching for nine years. She works in a nationally recognized suburban school district.

It is not hyperbole to say that the teaching profession in the United States is in trouble. Teachers are leaving the profession at rates that outpace retirements. Surveys indicate a high level of dissatisfaction, with only a slight majority saying they remain enthusiastic about their job. Teacher retention in public schools—a potential solution to the current teacher shortage crisis—has been on a decline since the late 1980s.

Research is incontrovertible on this point: experienced teacher turnover disrupts schools and negatively impacts student learning. Yet little is known about why experienced teachers leave, and conversely, how to keep them in the classroom.

Demoralized: Why Teachers Leave the Profession They Love and How They Can Stay challenges the common explanation of burnout to explain why experienced teachers leave their schools. It also offers lessons for teachers, school leaders, and policy makers about thinking more strategically about how to harness their talents to make a difference in the lives of students.

Drawing on ten years of research on teachers' moral concerns about their work, this book presents an argument that some forms of teacher dissatisfaction are better understood as demoralization. Demoralization offers a more precise diagnosis of experienced teacher dissatisfaction. Demoralization is rooted in discouragement and despair borne out of ongoing value conflicts with pedagogical policies, reform mandates, and school practices.

Not all teachers will experience demoralization. Some will not encounter situations that pose value conflicts between their job expectations and their vision of good teaching. Their values will be closely aligned with the pedagogical polices, mandates, and practices of their schools and districts. Some teachers approach their work from a perspective that does not emphasize the moral aspects of their job.

The preceding quotes provide just a sample of the types of moral concerns that contribute to dissatisfaction in experienced teachers who come to their work with moral motivations:

- failing to embody the values that have guided their practices for years
- complying with mandates that compromise their professional ethics
- contributing to student distress by following policies and procedures
- understanding that policies designed to support students render teachers expendable laborers
- realizing that the profession has transformed in ways that make career longevity unsustainable and unrealistic
- experiencing isolation when standing up in the name of professional ethics

While researchers show that teacher attrition is a process, not an event, most studies examine the experiences of beginning teachers and reveal only the earliest stage of the process. This book addresses the dearth of research on experienced teacher dissatisfaction and attrition. It draws on teachers' narratives as a means to raise questions about the concepts that are used to explain dissatisfaction among experienced teachers. These narratives offer insight into teachers' concerns that disrupt the common discourse of experienced teachers as resistant to change and primarily self-interested. Indeed, I show how these concerns are rooted in professional values of "client responsibility" and "craft performance" identified by sociologist Daniel Lortie and the desire to do "good work" as posited by Howard Gardner, Mihaly Csikszentmihalyi, and William Damon. Throughout the book, I chart how the feminization of teaching impacts the ability of teachers' moral concerns to be heard as ethical claims, rather than simply self-interested forms of resistance.

School leaders, policy makers, and teacher educators have been urged by researchers to inoculate and prepare teachers to withstand the perils of burnout with a strong dose of resilience.[1] While resilience is touted as a remedy to protect against teacher burnout, typically it entails adjusting to challenging situations by meditating, practicing mindfulness, and following other self-help recommendations. However, the process of demoralization occurs when pedagogical policies and school practices (such as high-stakes testing, mandated curriculum, and merit pay for teachers) threaten the ideals and values, the moral center, teachers bring to their work—things that cannot be remedied by resilience.

When teachers experience re-moralization—the ability to access and conserve the moral rewards of their work—it is through a more action-based approach that is tailored to the individual and the context in which they are working.

THE BACKGROUND

The seeds of this book date back to 2006 when a former coteacher sent me a copy of her resignation letter. Lisa had taught for twelve years, the last ten years in a large, comprehensive high school in San Francisco where I also taught for two years. We were both ninth-grade English teachers and collaborated frequently, eventually coteaching an elective together. I knew firsthand that Lisa was a fiercely dedicated teacher who was uncommonly effective in supporting student learning. Faculty members respected her, and she had assumed various leadership positions in the school and district throughout her tenure.

Having recently completed my doctorate, I read Lisa's resignation letter as a concerned friend and from the perspective of someone immersed in research on teaching. I noticed that Lisa's reasons for leaving did not fit into the categories typically used by scholars and educational leaders to describe teacher attrition. Lisa was a successful and passionate teacher who adored her students. A year or so before her resignation, I had visited her at the school where we had taught together. I didn't know her classroom number, but I was able to easily identify her room as I scanned the doors in the hallway. The room was filled with student work hanging from every surface and the hum of students working together. Hers certainly wasn't the only room in the school that had these qualities, but it was one of the few. I have a hard time believing that the quality of her teaching had deteriorated significantly in the next two years. My sense is that she was a better teacher than many up until her resignation.

In 2006, I could find very little research that addressed why teachers with five or more years of experience quit the profession. The most common explanation, especially for teachers who work in demanding, high-poverty schools, like Lisa's, is burnout. As I read the research, I developed an unsatisfying image of burnout: a candle with a finite amount of wick and wax. If it is never snuffed, the candle will burn out. Teachers burn out, presumably, because they do not ever take time to themselves by blowing out the candle of their teacher selves. As a result, they have no more resources (wick or wax) to offer their students and colleagues. Yet, Lisa still had plenty to offer her students and colleagues; she had not been extinguished prematurely. I did not see burnout as offering a sufficient explanation for Lisa's resignation.

Professor Susan Moore Johnson's team studying what they call The Next Generation of Teachers argued that teachers' career cycles had changed and new teachers no longer viewed teaching as a lifelong profession.[2] They argued that teachers leave the profession when they do not feel a "sense of success." Again, these explanations didn't capture Lisa's situation. Lisa was a teacher confident in her abilities. She had described herself as a "lifer." She could be heard warning her current students what she would reveal to *their* children when she was still working at the same school two decades hence.

Instead, Lisa explained why she was leaving the profession after twelve years this way: "I felt like I was becoming less good." For Lisa, this was a moral claim. Becoming less good did not mean that her pedagogical skills were waning. Rather, she offered an evaluation of who she expected to be as an educator and what she believed students deserved.

Lisa did not necessarily want to leave teaching, but she believed she could not continue to teach under the conditions she faced: a school that had once taught students in heterogeneous classrooms transformed into a rigidly tracked institution where students and teachers in the higher tracks enjoyed higher status and better resources; a small learning community that fostered teacher collaboration to provide supports to students was disbanded; scripted curriculum appeared on the horizon. The values of justice, inclusivity, and teaching as intellectually stimulating work that motivated her practice for over ten years could no longer be realized in the school that she also loved but that had changed so much over the last decade. She could no longer fulfill her vision of good teaching, even after making innumerable accommodations to new school and district mandates and organizational frameworks.

Lisa was leaving work she loved because she could not live up to the values that guided her practice. Working with the hypothesis that new federal policies, such as No Child Left Behind (NCLB), may be the reason that teachers like Lisa were leaving the profession, she and I embarked on a project in which we interviewed thirteen teachers with six to twenty-seven years of teaching experience in high-poverty schools who had taught before and after NCLB.

This book is written against the backdrop of interviews that Lisa and I conducted between 2006 and 2008 with experienced teachers who left the profession for moral reasons. I described them as conscientious objectors to teaching.[3] They could not continue to be complicit in practices that they believed denigrated the profession and that damaged students. In the analysis of the interviews, I developed the concept of demoralization—the inability to access the moral rewards offered and expected in teaching.

THE TEACHERS

The first set of interviews with conscientious objectors revealed that demoralization, like attrition, is a process. I hypothesized that if demoralization is a process, rather than an event, then teachers, school leaders, and their allies might be able to arrest or reverse it. I wanted to learn how teachers currently employed in public schools would describe the ways they managed moral concerns about their work. I wondered if the experience of demoralization need not conclude with teachers' resignations.

To better understand the process of demoralization and to find out if it could be arrested, I interviewed twenty-three teachers with five to thirty-five years of experience who had moral concerns about their work but who had not left.[4] I recruited these teachers via Twitter and through inquiries sent to teacher education programs, alumni networks, and associations such as the Consortium for Excellence in Teacher Education. While some of these teachers had only taught in the era of NCLB, all of them had experienced the introduction of the Race to the Top Initiative and the Common Core State Standards. Therefore, all the teachers in this study had worked through significant policy shifts.

The interviewees self-identified as having moral concerns about their work. As an exploration about professional ethics, I limited the interviewees to those who expressed moral concern about their own behavior and their colleagues', and excluded those who focused on the morals of their students.

Although any teacher can be eligible for demoralization, this book focuses on the experience of educators who have taught in public schools for five to thirty years. My purpose is not to ignore or diminish the experiences of early-career teachers who may have much to share about the process of demoralization. However, by limiting the research to those who had demonstrated their commitment to the profession through longevity, I was able to clear away potential confusion between disillusionment and demoralization.

The teachers I interviewed are not intended to be representative of the profession as a whole. Instead, their selected narratives provide insight into some of the ways that teachers have difficulty accessing the moral rewards of their work. They are cases that illuminate the concept of demoralization and provide examples of possibilities for re-moralization.

I asked the experienced teachers in my study what they understood to be good work, when they were able to best embody their conception of good teaching, and what prevented them from fulfilling that vision of their work. Often, I acted as devil's advocate. I challenged the teachers to justify their concerns. I proffered unsympathetic interpretations of their moral misgivings and required that they better justify their actions. I made these rhetorical moves only after we had established trust. Nevertheless, the arguments that the teachers developed in response to my critical probing showed that they were able to support and stand by their claims. Their responses provided critical details that might have been missing in their first articulation of their moral concerns.

At the time of the interviews, I would characterize seventeen of the teachers as experiencing demoralization. They were engaged in practices or contexts that contradicted or threatened their moral center as a teacher. However, I discovered that eight of the teachers had experienced re-moralization. They had been able to reestablish the moral rewards of their work without compromising their core values and ideals about teaching. All but one of the teachers were still teaching in 2017. Reggie was accepted into a prestigious doctoral program and resigned. All names, including those used in quotes, have been changed. Some identifying details have been altered.

I do not imagine a time when or place where teachers have no moral concerns about their work. The fact that teachers experience moral dilemmas in the conduct of their profession is not new, nor is it unique to teaching. However, the consistent finding from my research is that teachers' moral concerns about their work are rarely recognized as moral. As a result, teachers have few avenues though which to negotiate their dilemmas and no clearly identified resources to access in these challenging situations.

My hope is that this book generates discussion among educators about *their* moral concerns in teaching. More conversations about teachers' moral concerns will provide increasingly inclusive and wide-ranging insights into the many dimensions of demoralization and re-moralization in the profession.

ABOUT THIS BOOK

In chapter 1, I argue that any attempt to resolve the current US teacher shortage is incomplete without recognizing the moral sources of experienced teacher dissatisfaction. Richard Ingersoll has long explained and now Linda Darling-Hammond's Learning Policy Institute concurs that teacher retention must be a priority for US public schools. Given that many teachers enter the profession for reasons that could be characterized as moral, and that many teachers explain that they remain in the profession partly for the moral rewards, failing to understand the moral sources of teacher dissatisfaction presents a major gap in our understandings of teacher attrition. Teachers whose moral motivations sustain their work are susceptible to demoralization that may lead to attrition.

Without an accurate assessment of the problem, it is impossible to design appropriate solutions. In chapter 2, I distinguish demoralization, its causes and symptoms, from the phenomenon of burnout. Drawing on sociological and philosophical research, I show that the two main categories of teacher moral concerns are those that relate to harming students or denigrating the profession.

In chapters 3 and 4, I look closely at the two main categories of teachers' moral concerns: harm to students and denigration of the profession, respectively. The teacher narratives reveal the ways that teachers experience and negotiate moral concerns. In most situations in chapter 3, teachers are expected to follow policies and practices that they believe outwardly harm children or violate the trust that they have established with students. I also include two situations in which teachers are accused of physically harming students, and it is their school leaders' handling of this assumption that causes them moral distress.

Moving from a focus on students, chapter 4 homes in on teachers' responsibility to the profession. This chapter explores teachers' moral concerns about denigrating the profession, such as colluding with colleagues on dishonest grading. Another example involves a teacher who finds that she has unwittingly contributed to the martyr-teacher narrative that is so professionally and personally destructive. Members of a profession are responsible for maintaining the integrity of the profession. This chapter analyzes examples of teachers who feel they have failed to uphold the conduct required to fulfill this duty.

The call to cultivate resilience can often be understood as an expectation to better handle the adverse conditions that teachers encounter in their work. Chapter 5 offers specific examples of actions that the teachers took to re-moralize their work lives. Demoralization can be reversed, but re-moralization often involves transforming situations rather than accommodating them.

This chapter shows that teachers at any stage in their careers can become re-moralized. At times, re-moralization occurs partly as a response to the luck of new opportunities and changes in school leadership. Most often, re-moralization involves a meaningful connection with authentic professional community. The strategies that re-moralized teachers' work were almost never only an "inside job" that altered the educators' outlook or energy. Instead, almost all the teachers' experiences leading to re-moralization involved taking some form of outward action. However, these actions need not be *activist*. There are strategies available to those who are risk-averse, classroom oriented, or introverted, just as there are strategies that will appeal to those who are open to taking a public stand.

However, teachers are not the only persons responsible for their workplace. Chapter 6 provides examples of school leaders causing demoralization as well as serving as sources of re-moralization. School leaders need to be aware of the moral motivations that bring teachers to their work and provide opportunities for educators to articulate and navigate their moral concerns. A significant source of teacher demoralization occurs when school leaders refuse to recognize teachers' moral claims as moral.

Chapter 7 reveals the ways that teachers' unions can also be a means for re-moralization and the cause of demoralization. Uniquely poised to protect the integrity of the profession, unions can help teachers amplify their moral concerns and provide a collective voice for the significant moral work of teaching. Unions can connect teachers with an authentic professional community and provide outlets for taking re-moralizing action.

In chapter 8, I discuss the difference that demoralization makes. Reframing teacher dissatisfaction that stems from a moral source as demoralization enables educators to better understand and potentially transform their experiences. Naming the moral source of teacher dissatisfaction enables teachers to identify the origins of their concerns and to make clearer claims about their troubles. Mainly, the identification of demoralization versus burnout reveals that the problem is with the conditions of the work rather than with the teachers themselves. The book concludes with recommendations for systematic research that better isolates the moral sources of teacher dissatisfaction.

HOW TO USE THIS BOOK

For teachers who are troubled by their work, this book offers a new way to make sense of concerns about their practice and their profession. I provide action-based and collaborative examples of remoralization that can be set into motion by an individual teacher, groups of like-minded faculty, union organizers, or school leaders. Teacher educators will be able to use this book to discuss the common pitfalls and challenges practitioners will face in trying to live up to their commitments to teaching in the short term and over the long haul. Finally, I call upon educational researchers to fine-tune their inquiries to better capture the moral dimensions of teacher attrition and retention.

Research is incontrovertible on this point: experienced teacher turnover disrupts schools and negatively impacts student learning. *Demoralized* offers lessons for teachers, school leaders, and policy makers to attenuate the moral sources of teacher dissatisfaction. The book offers the following insights and recommendations illustrated by the narratives of experienced teachers:

- Teacher demoralization is often confused with burnout. The misidentification of the problem leads to ineffective remedies to address it.
- Moral concerns in teaching need be understood as matters of professional ethics rather than personal dilemmas.
- Demoralization in teaching threatens the moral commitments and values that sustain many teachers' careers.
- School leaders and unions can exacerbate and alleviate demoralization.
- Well-resourced, suburban schools are not exempt from reforms and mandates that have demoralizing consequences for teachers.
- Re-moralization is possible; most frequently, it entails cultivating an authentic professional community.

CHAPTER ONE

"We Have Been Taken Away from Our Own Reward"

THE MORAL SOURCES OF TEACHER DISSATISFACTION

Facing teacher supply shortages and high levels of teacher dissatisfaction, what should US public school leaders and policy makers do?[1] In response to these challenges, I anticipate that the public will be told of the need for more programs that attract the best and brightest young minds for short-term stints in the hardest-to-staff schools. We may be provided evidence that teacher education programs need to be redesigned to prepare teachers to meet the unique challenges of today's schoolchildren. Salary-based incentive programs that promise to attract talented individuals deterred by teaching's low pay may also emerge as proposed interventions.

Each of these proposed solutions responds to a particular problem with teaching: the low status of the profession relative to the education and training required for entry; demographics of teachers that are remarkably different from those of their students; low compensation relative to the preparation required for and demands of the work. These are recruitment problems. Interventions implemented along these lines are designed to harness a human resource stream into the teaching profession that might be diverted elsewhere.

As a longtime teacher and teacher educator, I know that these problems are serious obstacles to building a deep and diverse pool of public school teachers. The urgent demographic imperative to build a teaching force that reflects the diversity of the student population has been well documented. The low status of teaching in the United States cannot be attributed solely to its low pay; however, the low pay can be understood as a function of the profession's low status. The logic of the recruitment strategies described here could be termed the *Field of Dreams* approach: build it and they will come.

I have devoted my entire professional life to the practice, preparation, and study of teaching. I want teaching to be a field of dreams for those who enter it. Nevertheless, the attraction and recruitment logic misses an important component to the teacher shortage problem facing US public schools. This component is retention, especially for teachers who, despite its low status and low pay, have already proven their dedication to the profession.

Teacher retention is a problem, especially in the hardest-to-staff schools: usually urban or isolated, small rural schools where 30 percent or more of the students meet federal poverty guidelines for free and reduced lunches and the majority of students are from black and/or Latinx backgrounds. While these schools face challenges with recruitment, not having continuity among experienced faculty and school leadership is even more disruptive to building a culture of learning for students, as well as staff.

Teachers are leaving the profession at rates that outpace retirements and that create unstable conditions that undermine school effectiveness and student learning. Even if recruitment challenges could be resolved through short-term placement programs, the ongoing turnover of teachers (especially if the turnover is approximately every two years) is especially disruptive for students. Faculty with whom students develop close mentoring relationships move on, and institutional memory about students' life history and progress fades quickly. Members of the school community, savvy to the message of market forces, come to identify their school as a place where the successful get out if they are able. Therefore, those who do not leave are the "losers"—students identify themselves, their peers, and the staff who remain as losers. Why treat classmates and teachers with respect if operating with this collective self-assessment?

A similar phenomenon occurs with teaching staff. They may begin to internalize the loser identity if they continue to teach in a school with ongoing faculty turnover. However, not all will accept this self-deprecation. Even those who maintain a high-minded purpose for their role in the school may be overcome by turnover fatigue. Instead, they may experience a school in perpetual reconfiguration where norms are constantly being rearticulated and reestablished rather than refined and deepened. Schools that depend on a revolving cast of educators likely rely on imposed forms of authority such as highly regulated procedures and regimentation that students and researchers recognize as approaches consonant with the school-to-prison pipeline. Cocreated forms of authority rooted in interpersonal respect are nearly impossible to maintain under such conditions. The cycle thus continues: schools become rigid places focused on fear where neither students nor teachers want to be.

Places that have been traditionally hard to staff such as high-poverty urban and isolated rural schools currently feel the teacher shortage most keenly, but we cannot expect that the shortage will be confined to those locales. Well-resourced suburban schools are not immune to the impending staffing shortfall, but they will not be the first to experience the effects of high teacher turnover.

While wealthier suburban districts may boast higher salaries and well-maintained physical environments, this book shows that these districts may be taking on some of the characteristics that drive teachers to change careers.

WHY SHOULD WE CARE ABOUT TEACHERS' MORAL CONCERNS ABOUT THEIR WORK?

Facing a national teacher shortage that could exceed 100,000 educators by 2018, what should concerned colleagues, state policy makers, school and district leaders, professional unions, and teacher education programs do? One low-cost, high-leverage intervention would be to take action to retain teachers. Analyses of teacher employment data reveal that reducing preretirement attrition would virtually eliminate the current and anticipated shortage.[2]

High-achieving nations have about half of the annual teacher attrition rate that the United States is currently facing.[3] Richard Ingersoll has long argued that the teacher shortage needs to be understood as a problem of retention, not attraction.[4] Teacher retention in public schools has been on a decline for the last three decades according to figures published by the US Department of Education. While public school teachers moving between schools has remained relatively the same since the 1980s, teachers leaving the profession for reasons other than retirement increased from 5.6 percent to a peak of 8.4 percent in the 2004–2005 school year. The most recent figures are still high at 7.7 percent.

Yet, these nationally representative numbers do not tell the entire story. Schools serving high-poverty populations can experience yearly turnover as high as 25 percent. Arizona's Department of Education, for instance, reports that in 2014 over half of its districts and charters had between one and five educators break their contract or resign midyear in 2013–2014. In a time of shrinking school budgets and a recovering economy, administrators in Arizona report that better salary accounts for about 40 percent of their attrition. The majority of teachers leave Arizona schools for reasons *other than salary.*

The US Department of Education's national survey results indicate that the most significant reasons teachers leave the profession are "personal life factors" (38.4 percent) and "other factors" (20.5 percent). Although these two broad categories do not provide a fine-grained description of teacher attrition, these figures do debunk two popular, but erroneous, explanations for why most teachers leave: low salary and "fitness" for the work. Although popular wisdom and mainstream media often portray teachers as biding their time until higher-paying work comes along, reliable data show that low salary is not the most significant reason teachers leave.

National data reveal that most teachers leave due to "some type of dissatisfaction":

> Areas of dissatisfaction include concerns with the administration, ranging from lack of support to lack of input and control over teaching decisions; testing and accountability pressures; dissatisfaction with the teaching career; or unhappiness with various working conditions.[5]

Large-scale surveys, as well as the reports that they make possible, provide unassailable data to debunk myths and depict the magnitude and various facets of the problem with accuracy. They provide a rationale for new hypotheses to be explored and alternative policies to be enacted.

Linda Darling Hammond's Learning Policy Institute report reveals policy avenues worth pursuing. She also highlights well-publicized initiatives, such as fast-track certification routes, that may not resolve the "leaky bucket" teacher supply problem. For instance, the report finds that teachers with little preparation for the profession leave at rates double or triple those of better prepared educators. Therefore, identifying more shortcuts to the profession will prove shortsighted and ultimately ineffective. In contrast, identifying ways to make comprehensive teacher preparation affordable and rectifying profound disparities between teacher salaries in high-poverty, racially segregated schools and well-financed suburban schools could effectively target the disproportional attrition for teachers of color and the white teachers who work in those schools.

We still need more information about teacher dissatisfaction to develop effective strategies to attenuate experienced teacher attrition. Recent surveys report a "precipitous drop" in teachers' job satisfaction and an "undercurrent of despair" about their work.[6] Of the thirty thousand respondents included in the American Federation of Teachers and Badass Teachers Association's joint survey, 100 percent reported that they began their career enthusiastic about their profession. In 2015, only 53 percent said they remained enthusiastic about their work.[7] Given this extreme drop in teachers' enthusiasm about their work, it is imperative that we ask what accounts for this profound discontent.

Unlike many of the experienced public school teachers that I interviewed, Paul prepared in advance for our conversation. He's a scout leader, and I soon learned the many ways he lives up to the motto "Be Prepared." Paul occasionally reads from notes he generated in anticipation of our meeting. His frustration, tempered by Midwestern politeness, can be heard in the tremor of his voice.

Teaching is in Paul's blood. At least three generations of teachers preceded him, including his father, whom he describes as a "union guy." Paul was introduced to the idea of teaching as a calling in grad school but found the concept too weak. Drive, he explains, is a better way to under-

stand his purpose. Highlighting the priority that this drive occupied in his life, he describes transferring to a college that offered a different major to ensure that he would be employable as a language teacher. Finding his way into teaching took "tenacity, perseverance, [and] stubbornness."

Paul made strategic decisions that would enable him to build a life-long career in teaching. During his student teaching in an urban district, he witnessed the inverse relationship between student needs and school resources and the profound effect it had on teachers. Although he recognized that students served by that district needed high-quality teachers, he anticipated that he would burn out in four to five years. Paul attributes his seventeen years in the classroom partly to teaching in a well-funded suburban/rural district where students' basic needs are met, and therefore students come to school ready and able to learn. His school regularly appears in Newsweek's *list of the nation's top five hundred schools.*

Although the esteem of teaching has been degraded nationwide, the antiteacher rhetoric and policies have been particularly bitter in Paul's home state of Wisconsin. The passage of Act 10, a measure that eradicated collective bargaining for teachers as well as many salary scale benefits and tenure protections, demoralized Paul.[8] The new policies purportedly were developed in collaboration with practitioners and school administrators, but Paul feels alienated by what he believes should been a democratic process. He explains that "at no point do I find that my years of experience and expertise [have] really been valued enough for someone from that top level of government to actually talk to me, or even survey me." Paul views public schools as cornerstones of civic life and believes that teachers are public servants who should model and teach the virtues of democratic participation.

The defamation of teaching extended beyond the sphere of government offices and institutions. Paul recalls that many neighbors stopped speaking to each other as a result of Wisconsin's Act 10 that portrayed teachers as "Public Enemy #1." After more than a decade of going to the same barber, Paul felt that he was forced to make a change. He couldn't tolerate the relentless ribbing about being a teacher that he'd endure while getting his hair cut. Paul wonders aloud how members of a nation that can't treat each other civilly during a haircut will meet the pressing challenge of teaching all children equitably.

Teachers in Wisconsin are being asked to do more with less, even as they are being "attacked unilaterally" for having it easy and doing their jobs poorly. Paul heaves a packed three-ring binder that easily weighs five pounds onto his kitchen table. The binder contains a comprehensive and organized archive of all the materials from the state and district that relate to documentation that teachers must produce in the course of their work. The state has been rolling out initiatives and then revising expectations: his binder tracks various policy iterations and synthesizes what is actually expected of teachers at the present moment. He has also created step-by-step guides with screenshots for how to navigate the clunky and time-consuming online curriculum and assessment reporting platforms that the faculty are required to use. Paul shares these with his colleagues to minimize the duplication of effort.

Paul crescendos from incredulity to agitation, "We have been taken away from our own reward." The reward, he explains, was never about the money or even job security, although they were important benefits that Act 10 eviscerated. Teachers are separated from the reward of participating in and witnessing student learning and focusing on the improvement of their teaching. Rather than putting the emphasis on students and their learning, in Paul's experience, the state and district polices and mandates require that he devote the majority of his attention on bureaucratic details ("I'm a secretary.") that value seeming over being. The policies and practices reward individual teachers and schools that can "play the system," and this is intolerable for someone like Paul who sees his work as having dignity and integrity.

Paul repeatedly emphasizes that he is lucky to work in a district that values teachers and that attempts to render mandates meaningful to the goal of student learning. Even so, he recalls the countless and daily distractions that keep him from realizing the rewards of his profession: students pulled from class for testing, prep time lost while he proctored exams, meetings with so-called professional learning communities (PLCs) that are just small groups to roll out the latest top-down administrative mandate that entails even more paperwork, and the required use of computer-based applications that crash regularly and destroy work.

"My heart resides in teaching." The affirmations Paul receives from students and his parents sustain him. He recalls a parent who jubilantly threw her fists in the air when she found out that Paul would be teaching her younger child the following year. He finds satisfaction in the long-term relationships he develops with students, especially those who needed an extra push or ongoing support when he first worked with them.

Although scores attest to Paul's effectiveness in ensuring his students perform well on tests, these numbers do not reflect what really matters to him as an educator. Performance-based metrics that are now reviewed yearly by an administrator as part of the contract renewal process do not account for Paul's reputation in the community. Where can he account for the times he has let students know that he sees that they are not working to their potential, but he believes in them? Where can he show the times that he designs a learning activity that enables him to step back and watch the students take over?

It is not until we've spoken for nearly two hours that Paul reveals his shame. He tells me that the interview feels risky. I let him know that I am honored that he has trusted me with his account of the work he cherishes. Like nearly every other teacher I interviewed, Paul says that *it is cathartic to talk about his work—what makes it worth doing and what makes it intolerable. He feels heard, and that matters. A lot.*

We return to the shame: "I hate to admit this on tape. . ." Now that his job is no longer secure through tenure protections, he needs to ensure that his classes are fully enrolled. "I was more rigorous a few years ago. I've had to lighten up because if I don't lighten up, the kids won't take my elective."

Paul tells me his Catholic faith has helped him get through these times. His health has suffered, and his increased workload has eaten up the time he'd prefer to spend with his wife and school-aged children. "There's a good tired when you feel fulfilled at the end of the day. There's a bad tired when you feel drained from fruitless labor. Teachers, like most other professionals, want to feel purposeful and appreciated in their work. Such is the meaning of life: being purposeful and appreciated. We try our best to make our students feel this way, after all."

Compared to other teachers' experiences described in this book, Paul's transgressions may appear minor. He has not changed a student's grade when pressed by his principal. He has not colluded with other faculty to ensure that standardized test results appear better than they are. He has not assisted a distressed student during an assessment that forbade teacher intervention.

Paul's actions *as a teacher* in response to school, district, state, and federal policies and mandates cause him distress. This is the bond Paul shares with other teachers experiencing professional demoralization. He, like many of the teachers in this book, revealed his shame to me after deciding that I could be trusted. Shame is a moral emotion. It indicates something more than simply being dissatisfied. An expression or feeling of shame indicates that a person has transgressed a norm or violated a value that is an important part of how he or she identifies as an individual or as a teacher.

Another's assessments of the severity of a teacher's actions are inconsequential when identifying demoralization. Paul may feel shame about reducing the rigor of his classroom, whereas another teacher may not feel a twinge of guilt over something else that seems much more egregious. Paul finds the current condition under which he teaches nearly intolerable while other educators may consider them only inconveniences.

ADDRESSING DETERIORATING CONDITIONS

The nation's earliest teachers were often itinerant men seeking temporary work. Although the morally stringent and personally confining historical "rules for women teachers" are ubiquitous on faculty lounge bulletin boards, historical research reveals a more complex account of teaching in the nineteenth century. Women were able to pursue teaching as a means to establish independence, travel, and exercise their intellects.[9] Likewise, black men and women who worked as teachers were able to pursue higher education and establish middle-class status for their families while contributing to the education of their communities.

Since the 1950s, the status of teaching in the United States has experienced radical shifts. A brief review helps illuminate the challenges of retaining teachers of color and attracting high-achieving students from all backgrounds to the profession. While many accounts of *Brown v. Board of Education* depict the ruling as an unalloyed victory for racial justice, one of the many complicating factors of the decision was the effect on black teachers. When schools were merged as a result of desegregation ruling in 1954, black teachers were the casualties. Figures suggest that over thirty-nine thousand black educators lost their jobs as a result of *Brown*. The severity of this displacement for the profession and the deleterious effects on the black community's middle class cannot be overstated.

A more recent example of the active reduction in teachers of color is post-Katrina New Orleans. In 2005, the parish's majority-black schools had a teaching force with over 70 percent black teachers. By 2014, less than 50 percent of its teachers were black. At this same time, the proportion of inexperienced teachers also rose.[10] The disproportionate closure of schools that serve majority black and brown students may also reduce the ranks of teachers of color. More teachers of color work in high-need schools that would be subject to closure than in other types of schools.

The displacement of black teachers in the mid-twentieth century resulted in direct benefits for white teachers. However, the civil rights and women's movements that soon followed both dealt a blow to the teaching profession. Expanded opportunities for people of color and women resulted in a "brain drain" in teaching, especially when other professions proved more lucrative.

Teaching in the United States has traditionally been considered a feminized profession as a result of the educators' responsibility for children and the fact that the vast majority of public school teachers are women. Some attribute this feminized status as the reason that teaching has not risen to the level of full-fledged profession such as medicine and law. The level of professionalism for teachers varies widely by school type and student poverty level, especially in terms of teacher autonomy over decision making and pay.[11]

This feminized status also makes teaching an easy target for popular criticism. Refrains of teachers' lack of qualifications are legion, but titans of technology who drop out of school are lauded for their ingenuity. Teachers with experience are depicted frequently as ineffective and calcified, although perhaps dedicated, whereas individuals with long-standing careers in business tend to be portrayed as seasoned go-getters. The public's license to criticize teaching and teachers may be a result of its gendered status, but also affects its esteem.

The disparagement of teaching is felt keenly by those considering the profession as well as experienced educators. Gallup's *State of America's Schools* report describes the profession as "vilified." It describes the "alarming" findings that compared to twelve other occupations, teachers were the least likely to agree with the statement, "At my work, my opinions seem to count."[12] Teachers' ability to participate in decision making at their schools and their professional autonomy have been correlated to job satisfaction and retention.[13]

It is reasonable to wonder if teaching has really changed all that much. The profession has a longstanding history as "women's work"; salaries have mostly lagged behind other professions requiring similar levels of education; and, as public employees, teachers have always been required to meet the expectations articulated by local, state, and federal governing bodies. While these conditions have remained in place, demands on teachers' time, defining features of the work (standardization, recordkeeping), and scrutiny of teachers' daily activities (high performing and underperforming, alike) are unlike any other period in the history of American schooling. While teachers' work has changed, the organizational conditions in which teachers work have, by and large, deteriorated.

The deteriorating conditions for teachers have been documented globally and nationally and termed GERM, the global education reform movement. Following are some distinctive features of the last twenty years:

- standardization
- increased focus on core subjects/narrowing of the curriculum
- prescribed curriculum
- adoption of corporate practices/use of value-added measures
- high-stakes accountability for students and teachers
- fast-track or alternative teacher licensure programs[14]

The policy reforms ushered in by No Child Left Behind and that continue today were intended to improve the quality of teaching and learning for students who most need the support of a rich and engaging school experience. The tragic irony is that high-stakes accountability has been shown to have a "corrosive influence" on the quality of teaching and learning. The authors of a study on the detrimental effects of standardization, surveillance, and narrowing of all aspects of teaching offer a conundrum. They found that "strong teachers . . . offer the strongest defense against this corrosive influence."[15] Yet, retaining strong teachers becomes an increasing challenge in an environment where it is becoming more and more difficult to do good work.

Public school teachers are expected to do more with less; they are experiencing intensification.[16] Intensification refers to the increased professional demands added to teachers' workloads without concomitant time provided to incorporate new expectations or any reduction in previous duties. The new duties may include unprecedented expectations to collect and analyze data, recordkeeping to justify referrals to special education, explicit test preparation and practice, and adoption of new curriculum standards. While all of these activities may seem like reasonable expectations, those outside the world of public schools might be surprised to learn that it is not unusual for teachers to be provided no additional planning or administrative time for these tasks. Furthermore, teachers who want to incorporate new initiatives conscientiously are often frustrated when they are expected to incorporate new curricular mandates in short order without sufficient training.

Teachers may accept the intensification of their work when it is held out as a promise of professionalism.[17] For instance, teachers may believe that their ability to analyze data on student performance will elevate their professional status. Or, they may accept an invitation to contribute to curriculum development for the same reasons, without compensation or a reduction in their duties. Practices that deprofessionalize teaching can also result in intensification. Inexperienced and underprepared teachers may anticipate that a school's scripted and paced curriculum could make their jobs easier. However, these products may also increase a teachers' workload considerably given that they usually require many specific teacher behaviors, including highly regulated documentation of student performance and classroom displays.

Teachers in public schools have experienced deprofessionalization and intensification unevenly. Schools traditionally labeled as underperforming, especially those serving high populations of students of color in urban areas, were the first to see the adoption of many of these reforms. The global trend takes on distinctive features in the United States where decentralized, local control of schools is often seen as a point of pride by constituents on both sides of the political spectrum.

Some of the distinctive features of US-based reforms include:

- replacing locally elected school boards with appointed committees
- closing schools that serve predominantly black and Latinx populations
- diverting public funds into privately managed schools that seek to realize profits
- putting public schools and districts into competition for resources
- hiring school administrators with little to no experience in teaching or education

However, like Paul, not all teachers included in my research work in schools where it has historically been difficult to attract and retain excellent educators. Some are employed in districts that offer enviable salaries and where it is not uncommon for teachers to possess terminal degrees in their fields. In these cases, the challenges come from a rotating slate of school leaders, perceived disregard for teacher expertise, and a concern about the district's or school's uncritical adoption of policies and practices that the teachers believed were harmful to students or that undermine the work of teaching and learning.

The 2008 recession dealt a blow to public schools. Despite stimulus efforts, many schools lost staff positions. These positions included not only teachers, but also nurses, librarians, counselors, and paraprofessionals. While some schools inch closer to returning to prerecession staffing levels, many teachers now fill the gaps where support might have been provided by a nurse, a social worker, or a librarian. Teachers report that positions previously held by long-term, trained professionals are now being replaced with short-term volunteers with little to no preparation for the work.

Finally, teachers are concerned about meeting the needs of their students inside and outside of schools. Against this backdrop of increased curricular and performance-based expectations for teachers, the challenges facing youth in the United States are staggering. Over 50 percent of public school children are living in poverty.[18] Drug addiction and overdoses in many communities have reached epidemic proportions. A Southern Poverty Law Center survey reports that 80 percent of teachers have witnessed increased anxiety in their students as a result of the 2016 presidential election. Districts regularly provide training on creating trauma-sensitive schools and classrooms.[19]

INVESTIGATING THE MORAL SOURCES OF TEACHER DISSATISFACTION AND DESPAIR

Surveys of teachers' levels of satisfaction reveal clear links between deprofessionalization and dissatisfaction. However, uncovering the moral sources of teacher dissatisfaction requires a different sort of investigation. We know that improving teaching working conditions has been cited as a key feature of increasing teacher retention. However, the phrase *working conditions* includes "school environment factors that affect student and adult learning, including leadership, opportunities for collaboration, accountability systems, class sizes, facilities, and instructional resources such as books and access to technology."[20]

Undoubtedly, one strand of dissatisfaction can be connected to the deprofessionalization and intensification of teachers' work in an era dominated by GERM, or market-based reforms. This variety of dissatisfaction might be expressed by experienced educators as, "You're not paying me enough to do this job." Or, "You are asking me to do the impossible." Or, "My experience as an educator is ignored by this administration and these policies." These are all legitimate responses to deprofessionalization and intensification. These concerns also reference teachers' working conditions. They respond to the material conditions of the work: low pay, increased expectations in the face of reduced resources, and qualities of organizational leadership.

I hear a different sort of concern expressed when teachers like Paul describe how policies and mandates "take them away" from the rewards of the profession. My research indicates that *moral* sources of teacher dissatisfaction and despair contribute to the problems of teacher attrition. Moral sources of dissatisfaction may be more challenging to identify than dissatisfaction with material conditions, but they are an integral component of many teachers' satisfaction with their work.

Teaching in public schools necessarily entails a civic role and a responsibility for the well-being of others. For some teachers, a sense of justice, moral obligation, or care for young people or society provides a significant source of their motivation for the work.[21] As a philosopher of education and experienced teacher, I am especially attuned to hearing the moral significance that teachers attach to their practice. The teachers interviewed for this book incorporate at least one of two categories of "normative commitments" identified by sociologist Daniel Lortie nearly fifty years ago: norms of "client responsibility" and norms of "craft performance." Put simply, the teachers I spoke with discussed their beliefs about what students, their caregivers, and the community deserve (client responsibilities) and what good teachers should do and should not do (craft performance).[22] The terms *ideals* or *values* could easily be substituted for the terms *moral* or *normative*, as long as the ideals or values involve concerns for something or someone beyond the individual who holds them.

Here are a few examples:

- "We are doing an injustice to students if we don't share this information with them." (client responsibility)
- "I damaged the integrity of my work when I passed that student." (craft performance)
- "This testing is reducing education to test prep when we should be cultivating a love of learning." (craft performance and client responsibility)
- "How can I meet the needs of students when I am required to follow a curriculum-pacing calendar created by people who don't know my kids?" (craft performance and client responsibility)

I do not use the term *moral* to outline a particular set of behaviors that teachers must or must not exhibit. Good teaching comes in an infinite variety of forms and is responsive to local contexts and mindful of broader contexts. At the level of generality, this characterization of good teaching may appear to endorse relativism. However, as I highlight specific ways that the teachers featured in my research attempted to enact good work, I believe that their guiding norms will appear noncontroversial. Nonetheless, the choices they make to fulfill those norms may elicit disagreement. Conversations about these types of disagreements are an important function of practice-based professional ethics. I suggest that engaging in, rather than ignoring or silencing, discussions about professional moral concerns may prevent demoralization.

Sometimes the distinctions between statements that I am describing as other- or craft-regarding are difficult to distinguish from those that may initially sound as if they are self-interested or self-centered. I found that it was important to probe statements such as "I'm not allowed to be creative anymore," to learn if that statement contained any notions of client responsibility or norms of craft performance. Sometimes, simply saying "Tell me more about that" would lead to a fuller moral concern such as "I am not allowed to design and implement curriculum that builds on students' interests and questions." Other times, the response might remain at the level of the self-interested: "I really like studying frogs, but the new curriculum puts it in the third grade. My principal told me I can't study frogs again in the fourth grade." I suggest that school leaders who are interested in attenuating teacher attrition improve their quality of questioning to be able to discern the source of teacher concerns.

The differences between self-interested and moral concerns are sometimes subtle and may be intertwined:

- "I'm not included in decision making." (self-interested)
- "We emphasize the value of democratic decision making with our students, but teachers don't have a voice in decision making at our school." (moral: craft performance)
- "I can't be creative as a teacher anymore." (self-interested)
- "I am not allowed to design and implement curriculum that builds on students' interests and questions." (moral: craft performance and client responsibility)

In making the distinction between moral and self-interested concerns, I am highlighting the moral to reveal a category of concerns that require greater attention in order to gain a fuller picture of teacher dissatisfaction. However, my point is not to elevate the moral over teachers' self-interest. There are times when self-interest requires immediate attention, and there are instances when moral concerns are the product of paralyzing overanalysis. Only sustained conversations with teachers will reveal the difference. This book provides an opportunity to gain insight into the moral category of concerns expressed by a range of experienced educators in a variety of school settings.

On a survey, we would learn that all these teachers have "some type of dissatisfaction" with their "work environment." It is only through a finer-grained analysis that involves a conversation rooted in trust that we can access the moral dimensions of teacher dissatisfaction. Many teachers ask moral questions about their work: What does it mean to engage in good teaching? What should I do if my job expects me to violate norms and ideals that I believe are central to my work? Is it possible to be a good teacher for the long haul?

FINDING THE MORAL CENTER

The distinctive amalgam of what each teacher's beliefs about what students, their caregivers, and the community deserve (client responsibilities) and what good teachers should and should not do (responsible craft performance) composes the teachers' moral centers. I adopt the term *moral center* from Lee, whose experience is featured in chapter 2. Lee used the phrase to talk about the moral purposes of teaching that give her work significance. All the teachers I interviewed shared their moral center with me. I did not introduce the phrase *moral center* in any of the interviews. The teachers revealed their moral commitments about their work throughout our conversations, especially in response to these questions: What is good teaching? What does good teaching look like in your classroom? What prevents you from engaging in good teaching?

Moral centers are internal guides that help teachers gauge their distance from and proximity to the ideals they aim to embody as educators. Therefore, moral centers are revealed most clearly when teachers articulate their purposes as educators and when they fall short of them. Experienced teachers recognize that their ideals are best used as touchstones and self-evaluative tools, not easily achieved goals. The moral centers of the teachers I interviewed were compromised when previously attainable aspects of their ideals of good teaching were threatened or became impossible to achieve. Their moral centers were diminished when core commitments to their "clients" and "craft" were intractably compromised. These conditions can lead to demoralization in teaching.

The concept of *craft conscience*, coined by philosopher of education Thomas Green, is closest to my use of the phrase *moral center*.[23] Both concepts prioritize the moral commitments of teachers *qua* teachers. Likewise, both guard against idiosyncratic visions of good work. Craft conscience and moral centers are refined through experience doing the work in a community of practitioners. Nonetheless, I believe moral center better captures the ways in which the teachers I interviewed approach their professional obligations. Many philosophers believe that conscience is consulted only when something goes wrong. Therefore, craft conscience could be viewed as retrospective. A moral center, in contrast, guides teachers' choices and actions and enables retrospective analysis. Additionally, the image of a moral center conjures a more embodied, or gut, experience that rings more true to the way teachers in my study spoke about the role of their values in their work and the significance of their identity as educators.

MORE THAN A JOB

More than mere dissatisfaction, many teachers are in despair. Witnessing the loss of their profession and feeling powerless to stem its disappearance, they mourn and express many facets of grief. The teachers may be angry and desire revenge. They may broker compromises that leave them feeling betrayed. They may feel isolated and alone in their shame. Acceptance of the loss of their profession often concludes with their literal resignations.

The tremor in Paul's voice reveals the significance and depth of his concern about his profession. His concerns, like others quoted more briefly here, reflect issues that affect the core of who he has committed himself to be—as a person and as a professional. Paul, like many other teachers, experiences teaching as more than a job. It is a way to live his values. Some expressions of value or significance are "identity-conferring" commitments. These are the kinds of values that, if encroached upon, threaten a person's self-understanding.

Paul is not what we would call a workaholic, a person whose only source of satisfaction and meaning comes from his job and the recognition he receives through work. However, his work as a teacher has been one of the primary ways he has found to express his most significant commitments and to find the value he can bring to the world. For over a decade (well into the post-NCLB era), Paul had been able to enjoy the rewards of his work alongside the joy he finds in spending time with his family and his other forms of community engagement. Now, ten-hour school days are the norm. He makes it home for dinner and then goes back to work.

A man I suspect is not eager to find himself in need of a therapist, Paul tells me about the ways that his health and well-being have been compromised. However, it would be wrong to understand the problem simply as one of overwork. Paul is mourning the loss of his profession, which is different than simply saying that he has lost his job. Paul is still gainfully employed in one of the top schools in the country. Even so, he says he has been "taken away from [his] own reward." The blockage is more than simply a job being experienced as "less rewarding," it is the loss of a significant way Paul expresses his moral center.

What do we know about Paul's moral center as a teacher? He views his work as an expression of democratic values and as a service to civic life. He values holding high expectations for students while forming supportive relationships that push students to reach their potential. He has built a life in which doing this work well has been a goal and a priority. He knows that school is more than just academics, and he engages students by advising clubs and being an active member of the broader school community. He believes in fulfilling expectations set by elected officials and helping his colleagues do the same.

Recently, a suburban district nearby Paul's own experienced a 15 percent turnover in teaching staff. The costs of this level of turnover for districts, schools, and their students are staggering. Contrary to conventional, and short-sighted, wisdom, the costs are not recouped by the lower initial salaries of newer teachers. Paul wants to keep teaching until retirement. Labor statistics reveal that we need teachers like Paul to keep working through retirement.

This book offers insight and guidance for those who want to stem the personal and financial costs of teacher demoralization. It calls on teacher educators, policy makers, school leaders, and union organizers to take seriously the costs of compromised professional ethics. It presents an argument that demoralization is not a failure of individual teachers to develop professional resilience. Instead, teacher demoralization is an institutional and organizational problem that can be solved by drawing on the resources and information offered by teachers expressing moral concerns about their work.

The ways in which teachers experience demoralization share some common features of grief, but they may have distinct causes. The next two chapters focus on teachers' responsibility to students and the profession, respectively.

As the United States faces a teacher shortage, school leaders and policy makers need to know these truths:

- Much of the teacher shortage could be resolved by improving teacher retention.
- Many teachers bring moral motivations to their work.
- Moral motivations have been described as normative commitments to students and to the profession.
- When teachers believe that they must violate these normative commitments, they may express shame and experience demoralization.
- The moral sources of teacher dissatisfaction are not well documented using current survey instruments, and we need to gather better information about the extent of teachers' moral concerns.
- We do not need to wait for more data in order to address teachers' moral concerns about their work and to improve teacher satisfaction and retention.

CHAPTER TWO

"We Should All Be So Embarrassed"

DISTINGUISHING DEMORALIZATION FROM BURNOUT

Lee recognizes the signs of burnout: unrelenting stress, exhaustion met by sleepless nights, work that looms so large that it feels all encompassing. These were her feelings ten years ago when she worked as part of a team opening an alternative high school in the South. Unable to find a way to balance the demands of the job and her personal needs, she transferred to another school after two years. By switching schools, she was able to recalibrate the time she devoted to her job so she could also attend to her family and interests beyond teaching.

Burnout, however, did not accurately capture the growing unease, discomfort, and, frankly, shame she experiences at her current school. Lee explains that working at the alternative school shifted what she called her moral center, and this moral center began to guide her work as a teacher. At the alternative school, she collaborated with others who "were trying to craft the traditions of the school to make it feel like it had a really solid heart." Although the daily demands ultimately proved unsustainable for her quest for a balanced life, the mission and practices aligned with her beliefs about what good teaching should be: honoring the distinctiveness of each student; recognizing that students' cultural backgrounds and previous experiences profoundly shape their knowledge, interests, and learning; fostering student growth; and creating equitable learning opportunities.

The alternative high school principal is considered a visionary leader who places student well-being and learning at the center of all discussions and deliberations. He expected teachers to use professional development time to raise and discuss matters of importance to the school and to collaborate on classroom-level, team-based, and schoolwide plans to meet students' needs. Lee does not fault the principal for her approaching burnout. She recognizes that the demands of starting a new school challenged her own ability to set healthy boundaries with work.

Lee now works in a comprehensive high school where a professional culture of closed classroom doors prevails and where noninterference is considered virtuous. Some teachers have a lot of power and status by virtue of the school's complex hierarchy structure. Department heads tend to teach the highest-track classes and determine students' eligibility for honors and AP courses. They also fill the leadership vacuum in the main office by setting the professional tone for their subject areas. This arrangement leads departments to perceive collaborative overtures by teachers outside their subject area as an encroachment on their authority and autonomy. The building union representatives are drawn from the school's power elite and will fight doggedly for labor-related contract issues. Lee doesn't consider them allies and believes that self-preservation and the maintenance of the status quo are their primary purposes.

Lee did not leave her moral center at the alternative school; it is embedded in her professional ideals and identity. Each of the five schools where Lee has worked offered opportunities and challenges. At each one, she used her moral center as a touchstone, asking, "Can I keep doing good work here?" Sometimes, the ability to do good work entails ensuring that she doesn't burn out. At the alternative school, she could not continue to enact her moral center through her practice due to overwork and overcommitment. Her personal resources had been depleted.

These days, her ability to do good work has faced a different kind of challenge. Lee believes her moral center has become corroded. While a change of schools could keep impending burnout at bay in the past, she's beginning to wonder if she can continue teaching. Her current school's practices and policies render her complicit in what she views as harmful and unjust treatment of students. She believes that her role as an advocate for students is undermined by culturally insensitive and inequitable practices at her current school. She explains, "I was working with [newcomers] who were coming from places where they had experienced trauma or loss. And then they were coming into an environment that was tone deaf to that."

Even though she can stand by her teaching and believes she is doing her best to support students, she is troubled by her complicity in wrongdoing. She believes that her school communicates to newcomers that their identities do not matter, that they are outsiders, and that they are deficient. She feels guilty by association. She consistently communicates to students that they must take ownership for their learning and engage with the opportunities at the school, but, in her view, students encounter a school environment that alienates them and undermines those messages.

Many teachers find themselves at odds with longstanding school rituals that fall short of being adequately inclusive. However, Lee is deeply troubled by entrenched school practices that continue to confer privileges on white, middle-class students. Teachers of the honors track courses are permitted to develop their own prerequisites for admission. At Lee's school, students are required to complete an extensive amount of summer work in order to be eligible for honors enrollment. The prerequisites deter many students whose caregivers do not advocate on their behalf or who are unlikely to receive support with the summer work at home.

For incoming ninth graders, the transition to high school is fraught with new procedures that may be mystifying, especially for recent immigrants and refugees. Partly as a result of these eligibility requirements, the honors classes at this racially diverse school are made up almost entirely of white students. Enrollment in honors courses in Lee's academically tracked school not only increases the likelihood of college admission, but also of being nominated for leadership positions and enrichment activities. Missing out on honors enrollment in ninth grade sets a cascading loss of opportunity in motion.

Almost daily, Lee wonders how long she can stay in her job when she believes the school's environment subverts the values that inspire, guide, and sustain her work as a teacher. She cringes when she remembers juniors who proudly told incoming eighth graders that teachers hold honors students to a higher standard. The school's pervasive categorization of some students as "honors material" and others as less capable was a message that students internalized. The labeling was an affront to Lee's moral center as a teacher. She thought, "Oh my gosh, we should all be so embarrassed," but she looked around at a room of nodding heads. Later, she characterized her problem as "a fundamental conflict of belief systems."

In the face of these institutional practices that undermine the moral center of her teaching, Lee is teetering on the edge of quitting her job. Contrary to wisdom commonly proffered by other experienced teachers, Lee believes that the remedy is not simply to shut her classroom door. The legitimacy of her teaching is impacted by the school's culture and its *practices. "I have no one to go to in my school to discuss the things that I think are egregiously. . ." Lee pauses, then continues, recalling a teacher who consistently assigned an English language learner (ELL) student failing grades despite his solid grasp of content knowledge. "Well, the only way that I can think of it is malpractice."*

While some might characterize Lee's experience as burnout, I argue that her experience is better described as *demoralization*.[1] This form of professional dissatisfaction derives from teachers' inability to enact the values that motivate and sustain their work. Demoralization reaches its peak when teachers believe that they are violating basic moral expectations that educators should embody: do no harm to students, support student learning, engage in behavior becoming of a professional. *For teachers experiencing demoralization, the moral dilemma is not* what *they should do to be a good teacher, but that they* cannot *do what they believe a good teacher should do in the face of policies, mandates, or institutional norms. The source of the problem is the dissonance between educators' moral centers and the conditions in which they teach.*

Burnout is a common explanation for why experienced teachers are dissatisfied with their work. Undoubtedly, burnout is a problem that needs to be addressed, especially as the demands on teachers' time increase, their responsibilities expand, and the needs of students intensify. However, for many experienced educators like Lee, burnout does not capture the *moral source* of their dissatisfaction. We need a new concept to more accurately recognize and address this distinct form of teacher distress that can lead to isolation, despair, transfer to other schools, and to leaving the profession entirely. This new concept is demoralization.

When a teacher is described as "burnt out," this problem potentially could be resolved by the individual. Perhaps the teacher did not know how to set good boundaries with school leaders, colleagues, students, or their families. Teachers experiencing burnout may not have conserved their personal resources sufficiently, or perhaps they did not come to the job with sufficient personal resources that could act as reserves in times of difficulty.

In sources as diverse as parenting guidebooks, research on teaching, and seminars for business executives, *resilience* is defined as the ability to persevere in the face of adversity. Teachers also need to rely on resilience to navigate and sustain a career. Researchers and professional developers, however, have homed in on resilience as a silver bullet to address the teacher attrition problem. Resilience may be an important antidote to burnout, but it is an insufficient response to demoralization.

Here, I am building a case for the distinction between burnout and demoralization. Burnout signals that something is amiss with a teacher who could otherwise be doing good work in her position. Demoralization points to a *normative* problem the teacher sees with the context of the work. The teacher considers it very difficult, if not impossible, to engage in good work in her position. The source of burnout is an individual teacher's current psychological profile. Demoralization signals a problem with conditions of the work that impede the realization of the teacher's significant commitments and beliefs about the purpose and conduct of good work.

Sometimes, burnout is characterized as an unavoidable by-product of working in challenging schools or teaching students with overwhelming needs. These conditions may hasten burnout, especially in the absence of consistent school leadership and a stable teaching staff. When teachers find that they have reached the limit of what they are able to sustain personally and professionally, they may be experiencing burnout.

Demoralization can be a precursor to burnout. Experienced teachers who feel as though they can no longer do good work rarely make that decision based on a single incident. In every case in which I identified a teacher experiencing demoralization, the process was gradual and the teacher's responses along the way were substantial. When teachers' attempts to resolve moral concerns about their work are ignored, rebuffed, or ridiculed, it's possible to imagine that their personal resources may be depleted. Burnout may be an effect of unresolved demoralization. In this case, resilience is unlikely to help.

Quinn experienced four different mandated curricula in his last three years of urban teaching. He is exasperated because each attempt at standardization denigrates what he believes teaching and learning should be. Even if Quinn were given the authority to select and purchase his curriculum, he wouldn't take what he calls the "lazy" route. His moral center calls for teaching to be a highly relational, flexible, and responsive performance. Good teachers need to know their students very well and be tuned in to what is happening in their world. Was there a bake sale earlier in the day? Did a fight occur during gym? What's going on in the students' neighborhoods?

Quinn and his colleagues taught at a school serving the most challenging and highest-need students because they wanted to make a difference in their lives. They cared about providing nontraditional students with the support they needed to get a high school diploma. However, he describes working there as "not what teaching should be. It's not a healthy school." This assessment is markedly different from when he first started at the school and saw a dedicated and energized staff poised to meet students' needs.

Lacking schoolwide expectations for student behavior left teachers responsible for carrying the weight of moral dilemmas. If students acted out in class to the point of disrupting others' learning, Quinn had to deliberate between jeopardizing the relationship with the student and maintaining classroom-level behavioral standards. If the behavior rose to the level of asking a student to leave class, what alternatives were in place for a student whose presence at school was itself an achievement? He watched several of his friends and colleagues leave for other careers because they were so disheartened by the lack of support for teachers facing these dilemmas.

Quinn became the building's union representative when the person filling that position resigned. Although he did not have tenure, Quinn took on the role because he saw it as an important part of professionalism. The union enabled teachers to have a voice, and that was especially important in an alternative school where union work rules didn't align seamlessly with school practices. Quinn envisioned his role as informing the principal of teachers' rights and ensuring that those rights were respected. For instance, if the principal wanted to change the school hours, it could be done but required a faculty vote.

Once Quinn was affiliated as a union leader, his opportunities for other meaningful involvement in the school evaporated. Despite his interpretation of the role as collaborative, Quinn was no longer invited to participate in planning committees, and his relationship with his principal deteriorated. Quickly. Despite Quinn's bringing in a neutral teacher to attempt to repair the rift, the principal only saw Quinn's role as adversarial. Quinn received no additional pay or benefits for his service position to his school, his colleagues, or his union.

Anticipating an upcoming vote for the configuration of a special program, Quinn met with the faculty prior to their casting ballots. Examining each proposal, he guided the faculty through an exercise in which they imagined the pros and cons of each option. The secret ballot revealed that the faculty did not support the principal's preferred proposal. What happened next crystallized Quinn's decision to leave a school where he enjoyed teaching the students, was considered effective by his colleagues, and dedicated much of his free time to planning and service.

The votes were tallied during the school day. Quinn had learned that the principal's proposal didn't pass, but he wanted to focus on his teaching. Sharing the unpleasant news with his principal could wait. Word reached his principal nonetheless. Over the loudspeaker, as he finished up the last ten minutes of the day with his final class, the principal's voice entered the room. "I would like to thank Quinn Raymond for completely undermining the mission and goals of this school."

Quinn had given years of his life to the students and staff at the school. "Being a teacher is the majority of who I am. It's how I identify. It was a vicious attack on me professionally and personally. When that happens in any career, that's hard enough. You know, you're already vilified [as a teacher in public opinion]. It completely magnified everything wrong."

Some teachers who experience moral concerns about their work are able to intervene and make a change that restores their moral center. In these cases, teachers like Quinn are able to avert demoralization and burnout. Young and able to relocate, Quinn was hired at another school in a different city where his professional values aligned with the institution's mission. This time, he orchestrated a more mature job search, ensuring that the fit was right for him both in terms of the institutional values and the school leader's approach to management.

Lee had fewer choices when faced with demoralization. In her forties, with a family of her own and a strong network of relatives and friends, Lee's demoralization, if escalated or chronic, likely would have been remedied by a career change rather than relocation. Lee was invited frequently to participate in events at local colleges and was tapped by district leadership to participate in strategic planning, curricular development, and national conferences. Despite talent, commitment, and recognition, the chronic moral concerns that Lee encountered in her work could be the end of her career.

The path that might lead to the premature end of Lee's career could be averted. Teachers who experience moral concerns about their work do not necessarily become demoralized. However, untreated demoralization could lead to burnout. If the moral sources of teacher dissatisfaction are recognized and addressed, there could be opportunities to avert the current teacher shortage facing US public schools.

In the cases of Lee and Quinn, and any other teacher I would characterize as facing demoralization, the problem would not be resolved by individual remedies such as therapy, mindfulness, or resilience in the form of the ability to handle adversity. Experienced teachers know that teaching is hard and fraught with political and interpersonal challenges—sometimes outright conflicts. Demoralization is distinct from other forms of difficulty. *Demoralization occurs when teachers cannot enact the values that motivate and sustain their work. Their dilemma is not what should be done, but that they feel as though they cannot do what should be done.* It is unlikely that resolution to the dilemmas of demoralization will occur without some form of strategic action. The context may change by a teacher leaving teaching altogether, switching schools, or experiencing a fortuitous shift in policy, practice, or leadership.

Not all norms are good norms. Therefore, teachers need to be prepared to defend their professional values (their interpretations of the norms of client responsibility and craft performance) when they are challenged. They need to be prepared to offer rationales for their commitments and actions that are convincing to their colleagues, students' families, school leaders, and other stakeholders. Through this process, it is possible to critically examine norms and to revise them when needed. A sign of a healthy profession and of a responsible practitioner is the ability to provide good reasons and to be open to change when evidence supports a shift in belief and/or practice.

WHEN GOOD WORK IS THREATENED

Demoralization, as I am using the term, means far more than a state of being dispirited or even very depressed. It signals a state in which individuals can no longer access the sources of satisfaction that made their work worthwhile. Most teachers are unlikely to categorize the sources of their satisfaction as moral. Moral sources are any rewards from the job that cannot be explicitly seen but contribute to living a life that these teachers consider worthwhile and good. Moral rewards are also enjoyed when teachers believe that their work contributes to the right treatment of their profession, their students, and communities. When teachers use words like *conscience, integrity, dignity, guilt, shame, value,* and *responsibility,* it is likely that a moral concern is in play.

"Good work" operates as a moral evaluation that examines a profession's moral purposes and rewards. The focus of the assessment is not on the personal characteristics of individual teachers. Instead, it is the moral evaluation that teachers may make in reference to the work they do. Teachers' moral centers are articulated in the values and commitments they bring to and attribute to the work. The evaluation is not about outsiders assessing the content of a teacher's moral center. Rather, the assessment entails evaluating how well the values and commitments inherent to the work can be enacted in the work. This is a self-assessment undertaken by the teachers but that always references the imagined assessments of respected colleagues. Just like the "reasonable person" is often used as a test in legal proceedings, "admirable teachers" are visualized in assessments of good work.

The concept of good work comes from Gardner, Csikszentmi-halyi, and Damon's book of the same name. Their project examined the fields of journalism and genetics, two professions in the midst of significant transition and faced with major ethical dilemmas.[2] Individuals engage in good work when they believe (1) the work serves a social purpose that contributes to the well-being of others *and* (2) the way the work is conducted is aligned with that social purpose. In the fields of journalism and genetics, the inability to do the work ethically could damage the social purpose and might contribute to social harm.

Teaching provides many individuals an opportunity to engage in what they consider good work. Those who enter teaching today often select the career out of a desire to contribute something positive to the social world. Their focus may be on individual children, particular communities, the nation, or global welfare. For many who enter teaching with these motivations, the way in which the work is conducted is very significant. Therefore, altering the conditions and methods of the profession may be of great consequence for those who consider themselves as undertaking good work.

For teachers who pursue the profession from the perspective of undertaking good work, the rewards go far beyond the material to the moral. This is not to say that the material rewards are insignificant. Many individuals make a decision never to enter or to leave teaching because they need more than the material rewards that are currently offered, despite the appeal of doing good work through teaching.

The material rewards of the profession may become a significant aspect of teacher dissatisfaction if teachers engaged in good work can no longer access the moral rewards of teaching. The moral rewards of teaching are various and not experienced equally by all practitioners. Lee's moral center contains a commitment to creating a school climate of cultural inclusion. Although she could enact that commitment in her classroom, the moral rewards of fulfilling that commitment are compromised by schoolwide practices that make her feel complicit in creating environments that might traumatize and exclude students. Therefore, the schoolwide practices that go against her moral center as a teacher threaten and undermine the purpose and reward she has previously found in her work.

Nina's moral center, on the other hand, is guided by close observation of children and a belief that children will achieve academically if they are engrossed in their learning. When the curriculum was mandated, she could not allow the students a choice of topics or to respond to the energy throughout the day. She believed she violated her core beliefs about children and what they deserve as well as her purpose for teaching when she adhered to the curriculum. Following the rules led to a classroom that was joyless, for Nina and her students. The moral rewards for Nina were evaporating. She experienced demoralization.

Nina worked with the youngest of New York City's children, prekindergarten to second grade, for twenty years. She relished identifying the materials and designing experiences that would grab students' interests. She kept up with research on teaching practices. As a result, she found evidence to support her decision to give students choices about the direction of their learning for the day. Now, she is counting down the days until retirement.

An ardent supporter of public schools, Nina believes that the children who are educated publicly should have the same opportunities and quality of instruction as those in private schools. The lock-step pacing and focus on rote learning that was being mandated seemed antithetical to her. "They wouldn't dare educate [private school] kids the way these kids are educated." It is not only the methods and materials, but also the environment that compromises her vision of good work. After attending a workshop at a prestigious private school in the city, she thought, "Every kid deserves to be in a beautiful school. And then I'm in this. My school. And there's a mouse coming out during parent-teacher conferences."

Listening to Nina, I wondered if I'd encountered a teacher who could be characterized as passionate about teaching and her students, but who was rigid professionally. Was Nina a more palatable version of the teacher who dusts off the same yellowed lesson plans year after year? She kept speaking about how she would not follow some of the city mandates for her grade, especially in the language arts curriculum. I realized, however, that she described trying these interventions but then abandoned them if they "don't work." I wondered if she had given the different teaching approaches enough of a chance.

Our conversation is peppered with references to the many professional conferences she attends and the educational research she reads. She recalls asking her principal for permission to restructure her classroom in order to enact the new ideas that were generated at one of the conferences. Yet she refuses to enact the reading program mandated for her building. She has tenure and decided to prioritize student engagement over her own compliance. Her goal is learning, and she believes students will learn when they are engaged.

Finally, with the rollout of the Common Core State Standards, Nina feels as though she is being asked to move students into reading too quickly. So much of her moral center is supported by the work of Montessori and Reggio Emilia. Her reticence to push students to read does not seem to be rooted in resistance to change or to the evasion of difficult work. Nina takes the long view, and one that is rooted in research she has read. She is not focused on the level at which children read when they leave her classroom; she wants to help students develop into lifelong readers and people who thrive on curiosity. She believes that the scripted curriculum she is asked to deliver will undermine both of those goals.

Understanding why Nina was counting down the days to retirement is incomplete if we go directly to a diagnosis of burnout. Demoralization may be accompanied by some of the same emotions as burnout, such as depression, discouragement, frustration, and shame. What is distinctive about demoralization is that the previously accessible moral rewards of teaching are now elusive. Left untreated, demoralization may lead to burnout. Uncharacteristic of teachers who experience burnout, Nina still believed that she had a lot to offer students and the profession. The problem was that district mandates made it difficult, if not impossible, to do what she understood as good work.

WHO IS ELIGIBLE FOR DEMORALIZATION?

Any teacher may face demoralization, but teacher dissatisfaction of this variety can be more precisely identified in experienced teachers. Teachers with tenures of five or more years have demonstrated a degree of commitment to the profession, can articulate their vision of good teaching, and can describe in detail the ways that they have been able to enact their visions and values over time.

Any teacher may experience demoralization, but some are more prone to it than others. Teachers who come to their work with significant moral purpose or those who operate with a strong sense of professional ethics are more likely to experience demoralization than teachers who have a more functional approach to their work.

Teachers earlier in their careers may be testing the waters to see if the profession aligns with their interests and skills. True in most any profession, new teachers anticipate what the work should be like. These expectations may relate to the so-called theory-practice divide, but also include romantic idealizations of the role and blind spots about major components of daily work. Focusing on more experienced educators has enabled me to distinguish demoralization from early-career disillusionment.

Disillusionment comprises the experience of most individuals moving from a preservice mode to active service. We all build a vision of what our classroom will be and what our colleagues will be like during the preparatory modes of our work, regardless of how substantial or abbreviated that preparation may be. We necessarily develop a positive vision, even if it right-headedly anticipates challenges. Otherwise, we would not move toward the challenge. Disillusionment is not just a by-product of naïve fantasies that fall away, but a necessary component of moving through experience.

Teachers who experience demoralization are able to point to a time when they were able to enact the values that motivated and sustained their work. There is a before and an after to demoralization. Unlike disillusionment that may provoke a teacher to say, "I realize that I will never be able to do x. . .," demoralization involves a teacher saying, "I once was able to do x as an essential component of my work, but now I cannot."

Outwardly, demoralization may seem remarkably similar to burnout. Exhaustion, disappointment, and frustration may be just a few of its manifestations. However, the *source* of the symptoms makes all the difference in the diagnosis and treatment of the problem. The current fascination with building teacher resilience is an apt response to burnout but ineffective for addressing demoralization. Burnout is a depletion of personal resources that makes the act of teaching intolerable or unsustainable. The source of burnout is located in the individual psychology of the teacher who cannot find balance, maintain sufficient boundaries, or withstand the emotional demands of the work.

The inability to access the moral rewards of teaching may not be the result of a lack of personal fortitude or a wavering moral sensibility. Rather, we need to look outward to the teaching contexts that may make it difficult for practitioners to engage in good work. To better understand what conditions contribute to demoralization, the next chapter looks at the ways that good work is undermined when teachers believe their work harms, rather than helps, students. Chapter 4 examines the ways that good work is challenged when teachers believe they degrade the profession by following the mandates or implicit expectations of their jobs.

In contrasting demoralization with burnout, this chapter showed:

- The emotions associated with demoralization are often misunderstood as symptoms of burnout. These can affect:
  - feelings about their profession;
  - consequences for their health;
  - impact on their families;
  - relationships with students; and
  - expectations for their longevity.
- Individuals who see teaching as a way to do good work are more prone to demoralization than those who approach the work from a more functional perspective.
- The dilemma in demoralization is not a question of what should be done; the problem is that what should be done is not possible.
- Demoralization is a problem with the context of teaching, not the psychological well-being of the teacher.
- Demoralization is not an inevitable by-product of teaching.

CHAPTER THREE

"They're Suffering and They're Struggling"

SOURCES OF DEMORALIZATION: CAUSING HARM TO STUDENTS

T esting became increasingly high stakes for students as well as teachers in Hilary's southeast state. Hilary's son attends the school where she has worked as a media specialist for twelve years (she completed her first year of teaching at another school). She is concerned about his level of anxiety. In a school labeled one of the nation's best, she didn't see this coming. Her school avoids the relentless test prep and drill that she knew occurred at lower performing schools. After a bit of investigation, Hilary learned that word had drifted down from her son's friends' older siblings. They told the third graders that how they performed on the test would determine if their beloved teachers would keep their jobs.

Hilary believes that the tests also have outsized implications for students' futures. As early as the fifth grade, placement decisions are made based on test scores and grades as a result of the district's choice plan. Despite the potential significance of the exams for students (through placements and promotion) and teachers (through VAM [value-added measure] calculations and merit pay), the state-mandated tests must be administered regardless of the conditions students are in when they enter school. She illustrates with a scenario. If a student walks into school distraught after witnessing her parents fight that morning, Hilary believes it would be absurd for her to ask the student to sit down and take an exam. That is precisely what the state requires: if the child is in school, she must sit for the exam.

By following the mandates of the state, Hilary may violate her moral center as a teacher. If Hilary administers the test under these conditions, she may signal to the student that her problems at home are inconsequential. Sending that message while following state mandates violates Hilary's commitments to care for the social-emotional, physical, and academic needs of the child. She may feel that she is violating trust that she worked to establish with the student. Hilary's professional integrity is also disregarded. She knows that the exam results may underreport the child's level of competence if taken under conditions of distress. The poor performance could be a problem for the student (possibly limiting her school placement options), the teacher (potentially contributing negatively to her VAM), and the state (receiving data that may be faulty).

When she follows the rules, Hilary goes against what she believes is right. She is caught between responsibility to her employer and the citizens of her state (assuming that the policy's makers were democratically elected), and her professional standards that include duties to care for and act in the best interest of children. The pressure builds as she describes the impossible position she occupies. "It's just so frustrating!

Ahhh!" It's one of the few times Hilary raises her voice in the three hours I spoke with her.

Hilary describes herself as a person who has always held herself to high ethical standards. When she worked in another field prior to entering teaching, Hilary was dismayed by her boss's creative interpretation of regulations. "I'm not that person. I, I can't break the rules or see how far I can get away with things." She believes that it is essential that she follow the clear mandates and procedures set by her school, district, and state. Yet, following the rules could make her very uneasy.

The hypothetical situation Hilary posed seems almost trivial in comparison to the actual situation that still haunts her. This is her shame. In the library, she proctored an exam for a small group of students who were given extended time due to their 504 or Individualized Education Program (IEP) plans that ensure that students receive accommodations due to disability or other needs that require learning support. One fifth-grade student with cerebral palsy who used a wheelchair was part of this group. Computer-based testing had become mandatory for the state exams, but the student had never been tested using a computer.

Before computer-based testing was implemented, the student's teacher would fill in the answer bubbles for him. Now, it was a physical challenge for the student to move the mouse. Additionally, to answer problems, he had to manipulate various objects and engage in multiple steps. Hilary is visibly rattled as she recounts this incident. "It was a test that took all of our other students 160 minutes over two days. [It took the student with cerebral palsy] ten hours [to complete the exam] over two days. That just doesn't feel right to me. Watching him struggle with the mouse to drag the ruler tool over. It's very fine motor skill stuff that a kid with cerebral palsy struggles with. And there's not a thing we can do; there's no alternative."

She continues, highlighting the violation of trust she committed while following the rules. "This is a kid I've known since second grade, so this is the fourth year I know you. I have a relationship with you. It bothers me. I would not want to see my kid in that position. I certainly don't want to see anybody else's kid in that position where they're suffering and they're struggling. And suffering is a really harsh word, but I don't feel like it's overused in this instance."

Students should experience productive struggle, Hilary believes. She does not think school should be effortless or an easy experience at all times for students or teachers, for that matter. Critics of the math section of the Common Core claimed that early elementary school students were asked to engage with mathematical ideas that were developmentally inappropriate. Bottom line: it was too difficult for young kids, claimed some teachers and parents who didn't understand the new approach to math.

Hilary believes that young children should be exposed to foundational concepts in math and encouraged to grapple with abstract problems, even if they would not grasp the material fully. Going through the reflective process of earning her National Board Teacher Certification helped Hilary see what students could be capable of when they were appropriately challenged. She suspected that teachers and parents were primarily reacting negatively to change. They were expressing their own worries about moving into new curricular and pedagogical territory.

Seeking ways to connect with innovative peers and experimenting with new ideas have been hallmarks of Hilary's thirteen years in teaching. If she encounters a problem, she reaches out to her professional network and seeks their advice. When a claim was made about the purpose of VAM, she read up on what educational researchers have identified as statistically problematic. After encountering polarized perspectives on state policy, she joined a group that focused on finding common ground. Facing a change in leadership at her school, she investigated strategies for transitioning to a teacher-led governance model.

The testing issue feels harmful and immovable. Hilary can't find a way to reconcile her duty to administer exam after exam with the negative outcomes of narrowing the curriculum, closing libraries and computer labs for weeks, and diverting school resources that could be used to enrich students' experiences. She is nagged by the ways in which testing dehumanizes students and teachers by providing few ways to respond to individual needs and particular circumstances without flouting the law. "Equal is not always fair," says Hilary, "And that bothers me."

Teachers across her district decided to gather regularly to support each other. Hilary applied to and was accepted into a national organization that supports teacher leadership and provides training and platforms for teacher voices. These professional learning communities and opportunities for further development have been integral to keeping her in the classroom. The winner of a school-level teacher of the year award and, more recently, formal recognition from the state's governor, Hilary was considering leaving the profession a few years ago.

Hilary emphasizes that teachers need to be able to grow and advance in their careers without leaving the classrooms they love. This intervention on the relatively flat career trajectory of teaching is incredibly important. However, I also hear the opportunities these professional communities have provided Hilary to make sense of and respond to some of the moral concerns she has encountered in her practice. These leadership roles have offered a route into action that staves off the hopelessness of demoralization.

This chapter examines how experienced teachers describe the causes of demoralization in their work in relation to students. Many teachers enter the profession to advocate for and empower students. The moral dilemma these teachers may encounter is not "What should I do?" but "I know what I should do, but I am told I must do something that harms children." In this category of demoralization, teachers usually cite the ways that they were told to engage in practices that they believed were developmentally inappropriate, pedagogically ill-advised, or damaging to students' social-emotional well-being.

Research reveals two characterizations about teachers. The first is that most enter teaching out of a desire to improve others' lives or due to an affection for children. The second is that teachers tend to be rule followers. There are exceptions to every generalization, of course, and we know that secondary school teachers may be more motivated by their subjects than their students and that their personality profiles are slightly more prone to rule breaking than elementary school teachers'. Nonetheless, the typology of public school teachers holds: generally, they are people who are rule and law abiding and they care about kids.

This personality profile, while possibly serviceable for teaching in other times, places teachers in a bind. Teachers are told that the policies and practices are enacted for the good of children. Teachers, by and large, want to do what is good for their students and to be in compliance with the expectations outlined by their supervisors. However, when educators witness the negative outcomes of following the rules for their students' learning or well-being, they face a dilemma. How can they fulfill both of their obligations?

Teachers may experience cognitive dissonance when they are told that in order to provide students with the education that they deserve, they must do things that appear to harm the students in their classrooms. While Hilary has not drifted into demoralization, the potential is great for teachers who feel as though they have no voice.

Authoritarian school leaders who demand compliance without dialogue may silence teachers' voices. However, teachers' voices may be muted in other, more insidious, ways. Exhortations to "leave no child behind" or to ensure that "every student succeeds" position the mandates that emerge from those policies as inherently good and in the service of children and society. Teachers' concerns leave them open to criticisms that they are not willing to contribute to the betterment of society, or that they are satisfied with leaving some children behind, or not interested in helping every student succeed. The ways policies are written may exert a powerful moral force designed to be visionary and inspirational as well as to quell criticism. School administrators, curriculum consultants, and legislators can draw on this irrefutable policy language to enforce compliance through moral manipulation. For teachers like DeeDee, a thin interpretation of professional community may lead them to betray their expertise and moral centers.

DeeDee's personality aligns closely with the profile of a rule-following teacher who loves children. I considered her the most self-effacing teacher I have ever met, especially when her extreme humility stood in stark contrast to her credentials and awards. Although DeeDee might be an outlier, many teachers underplay their expertise.

A teacher with thirty-five years of experience, DeeDee worked in a small, well-supported rural elementary school in New England for her entire career. She had won multiple state-level awards for her excellence in teaching math to young children, and she received a teacher of the year award from a multinational nonprofit. She also was a certified instructor for a nationally recognized approach to math that emphasizes student discovery through manipulatives and understanding of concepts. She continued her education through reading practice-based research such as Jo Boaler's work at Stanford University and taking online courses.

A former principal, whom DeeDee respected a great deal, determined that it was necessary for the entire school to use a single publisher's textbooks for K–6 math instruction. This decision came on the heels of new data collection suggesting that students were not scoring well enough in math. Although DeeDee doesn't remember it this way, it seems to coincide when the federal government offered funding for "research-based" instructional materials as a component of No Child Left Behind.

The principal empowered the teachers to work together to select the textbooks from a selection of three or four mathematics textbook publishers. As someone already highly trained in mathematics instruction, DeeDee had strong feelings about the options. Yet, she remained silent when her colleagues selected a series that provided a step-by-step teaching manual. She muted herself purposefully out of a desire to be a team player. DeeDee recognized that her colleagues did not have as strong a pedagogical background in math as she did and needed the support of the manual.

The years went on, and DeeDee attempted to teach from the textbook to be a team player. All along, she felt sick inside. She knew that she was not teaching to the best of her ability. "At one point, through tears," she explains, "I went to the principal and explained, 'I can't do this.' Anybody can come in and turn the page. And he quietly came to me at one point and said, you don't have to use the book, but don't tell anybody. And I felt like that was not fair. I have to do underhanded things because you don't trust [my colleagues] as much as you trust me? And you really don't trust me any more than anybody else, but I'm making waves!"

DeeDee was mortified that the principal's demand for uniformity involved a request for her to be duplicitous with her colleagues. Yet her *real anguish could be attributed to how her lackluster math instruction affected her students. She recalls, "The word* fidelity—*that was the big f-word in my mind! You know I hated to go to meetings where they said were going to 'use this with fidelity.' Come on! Can we watch kids with fidelity instead? Can we watch and see what they need and [help them to] grow from there?"*

The effects of teaching the textbook with fidelity demoralized DeeDee. Gone were the days when her students named math as their favorite subject. She felt dead in her teaching, and she worried that by teaching with the textbook, she lost the ability to help students fall in love with math and explore its concepts more deeply. "I left my soul out of the picture for a few years. That's an easy way to say it. My passion was gone. My teaching soul was gone. It was almost like that drugged feeling where you just do what they tell you to do. And you don't have any fight left in you." She planned on just following the rules and distancing herself from the work she was doing. It hurt less that way. Retirement wasn't too far off.

DeeDee's demoralization could easily be the final, and tragic, stage in a life-long teacher's career. Fortunately, for DeeDee and her students, she offers us an example of a veteran teacher whose work can be re-moralized, as we will see in chapter 6.

Teachers like DeeDee encounter a terrible dilemma: as a dedicated rule follower, she is trapped because she knows that the rules that she is following are not serving students well. Furthermore, the repetitive language of fidelity made her feel as though she had been lobotomized as a teacher and that it was her students who suffered the most. The combination caused her to lose spirit, hope, and pleasure in her job. She experienced an inability to access the moral rewards of her practice. Only by generating a thicker understanding of professional community did she find a way out of the bind she experienced with fidelity to the textbook.

Being a team player for DeeDee initially meant following the rules set by her administration. It also entailed submerging her professional expertise when faced with her colleagues' discomfort with teaching math. However, when empowered by a principal who placed trust in teachers and a researcher doing subject-specific observations, DeeDee imagined a new role for herself among her fellow teachers. Colleagues had remarked on her dissatisfaction and asked, "Does it really matter at this point, DeeDee?" While some teachers with thirty-five years of experience might be willing to bide their time, DeeDee thought, "Yeah, it does. I didn't know it did until they asked that question." DeeDee realized that it mattered: she wanted to conclude the final years of her career teaching in a way that served students well and that honored her expertise. She thought, "I'm supposed to be part of a team, but I [began to wonder]: Can you be part of a team in a different way? Can you have yourself back? Can you have your soul back?"

DeeDee moved from a place where she had ceded her professional responsibility to a new orientation where she could embody and enact her professional responsibility. Even though DeeDee would likely recoil from this description, she became a teacher leader that day. She was able to articulate and stand by her moral center as a teacher and to help her colleagues see why that mattered. "I started making plans in my mind that I can be me again. For the little bit of time I have left because I know it's not that long. I'm going to be sixty this year. I'm not the little person that I used to be. I'm still crawling around on the floor, but it's not easy. It's a little hard to get up!"

Unlike DeeDee, Gavin found a way to articulate his moral center early in his career. Five years into teaching, he started an online movement that called for teachers to articulate their core beliefs about teaching in the face of an onslaught of reforms that seemed insensitive to children and their needs. Although Gavin taught in a large metropolis known for advocating standardized approaches to reform, he was able to make incremental changes that ultimately proved transformational for the well-being of his students.

Gavin's impulse to engage in social justice emerged while in college, but his professional moral center was shaped by a teacher education program that articulated a clear set of values. He sought out a graduate program with a clearly articulated philosophy statement. One of the most significant of his values is that children receiving special education services should not be segregated from other students. His moral concerns were activated when he was offered a position at the school where he continues to teach. Although he thought he was interviewing for a mixed-mainstream classroom, he realized that he was being considered for a self-contained special education classroom when the secretary told him how many students were in the class.

Even though he was a junior member of the faculty, Gavin attempted to intervene on school practices that he believed were harmful to children. Due to the low skills of many students receiving special education services in his class, Gavin was placed on a planning team that was two grades below the age of some of his students. He advocated that he plan with the grade-level team appropriate to the age of his students.

Soon, Gavin began collaborating with a member of the grade-level team to combine classes and trade off teaching mixed-mainstream and special education sections. Eventually, they officially team-taught a single mixed-age class.

"All students should be together with all students. It's all one group of human beings," explains Gavin. "From the kids' point of view, I absolutely saw the isolation that they were experiencing. I feel that the social

isolation was complete. They were understanding that they were being seen as different." Gavin recalls a situation when his special education students from the self-contained classroom had been wrestling with each other on the playground. Gavin tells me that *"Keshawn was just really, really visibly upset. He told me, 'Kids are looking at us like there's something wrong in our faces.' He was articulating that you're different or you're doing something else so wrong that he was actually perceiving that there must be something wrong with his face."*

Knowing the overrepresentation of students of color, especially black boys, in special education, Gavin took prior assessments of students' capabilities as a snapshot that required more evidence. He believed that there was a good chance that his students could do more than what was revealed in a special education file.

Gavin returned to a principle that many special educators may know: operate with the least dangerous assumption. This principle asks more of teachers than to identify the least restrictive environment as federal law requires. It demands that teachers engage in imaginative displacement and consider what the effect of an assumption, and the actions and decisions that may follow, may have for a student today and into the future. Gavin was clear that he would rather be wrong erring on the side of inclusion than living with the potential damage that could result from the social isolation these older elementary school students experienced.

Working from the principle of the least dangerous assumption enabled Gavin to meet the needs of individual students as well. A girl in his class with selective mutism was being evaluated for special education services. Worried that others on the child study team might assume that she had low cognitive capabilities, Gavin sought ways to enable Nilda to demonstrate her understanding. Although she could, and would, read aloud, she could not demonstrate an ability to draw on the text to support her answer.

Gavin noticed that Nilda would become animated if working with a small group. He had a hunch that he could gather evidence of her ability to make sense of text if he were not present as an evaluator. "So I said [to Nilda's group], 'Go out into the hallway and plan out your whole project.' They got started and I said, 'And I'm just going to put a camera here, because I'm doing guided reading [with another group] and you can do your independent work.' Nilda spoke the entire time. She showed the attitude of the character that demonstrated that she actually understood the deeper aspects of the book. She added all of this dialogue that wasn't just pulled from the text, but it included her interpretation."

This fierce commitment to finding ways to demonstrate what students know and to fostering student well-being came to a head with federal- and state-mandated testing. For the first few years of his work, Gavin administered alternative testing that included portfolios and performance tasks. Then, working in a mixed-mainstream and special education class, he had to administer tests associated with the Common Core State Standards.

Kids from his class sat through [the tests] saying, "I feel like a dummy. I feel like a stupid dummyhead." Some broke down, put their heads on the desks, and sobbed. Gavin felt wounded because he was contributing to students' distress. He explains, "I had built a relationship with the kids that I would always give them work that I felt was within their capabilities. In other words, at a level that they could access. I felt like I was betraying them. That I was saying that [giving a test that was several grade levels above what they could currently do] was okay . . . As a person that works in an institution, or a school, I have to feel confident that it's in some way rooted in an ethic that I can stand behind and that I can feel that I can do the work that I'm comfortable with." Ultimately, Gavin took a stand with other teachers in his school and refused to administer the state examinations.

REBELS, RULE CHANGERS, RULE FOLLOWERS, AND RECLUSES: PART I

Teachers who have moral concerns about their work may deal with these problems in a multitude of ways. I have written about teachers who quit their jobs as conscientious objectors, but not all teachers have the financial or personal means to take a stand in that way.[1] Likewise, not all teachers' moral concerns necessarily rise to the level of resignation. While published statements—"quit lit"—and public stands make news and may go viral on social media, teachers find various ways to cope with moral concerns about their work. Some will make a full-frontal attack that, while not public, may entail significant risks. These rebels may risk their jobs or the good-will of their school leaders. Rule changers make efforts to alter the policies or practices with which they disagree. Rule followers enact and enforce mandates despite their deep misgivings. Recluses may shut the door and do what they think is right.

Were they all working in the same school, Hilary, DeeDee, and Gavin might not be teachers who would gravitate toward each other in the teachers' lounge. They might find themselves at odds during discussions about new pedagogical policies during a professional development day. They might even avoid working with each other if required to participate in a mandated and preas-signed professional learning community. Nonetheless, they share in common a concern that by fulfilling the expectations of their work, they are harming children.

Hilary's criticism of high-stakes testing reflects her concern for the social-emotional welfare of her students. She witnessed students, her own high-achieving son included, becoming increas-ingly anxious over their performance on the state tests and how their performance would impact their teachers. Hilary was troubled by her role in upholding policies that subjected students, like the young man with cerebral palsy, to testing conditions that seemed dehumanizing. Accommodations that enabled him to take more time did little to alter a situation presenting physical challenges that tested his motor skills, stamina, and determination more than his subject matter knowledge.

Deeply engaged in educational policy and comfortable with the role of a public figure, Hilary is a rule changer. She writes blogs that have been picked up and republished by national outlets, she seeks out opportunities to collaborate with other stakeholders to revise state laws, and she is developing a plan to start a teacher-led school. In the meantime, she is also a rule follower. She reveres authority and wants to stay on solid, rule-following ground so she can remain credible and beyond reproach while advocating for change.

DeeDee's concern about the mandated use of textbooks could be read by some as a resistance to adopt new curriculum. However, because she is an accomplished and recognized innovator in math teaching who continually seeks out new opportunities to learn, this characterization does not seem apt. Instead, I interpret her criticism of the textbook as reflecting an awareness of the pedagogical and curricular methods that serve students best. This concern for her students becomes clear when she comments that her students once named math as their favorite subject, but few did when she toed the line with her colleagues. DeeDee cares about the intellectual engagement and achievement of her students and believes that she was committing a form of malpractice by going through the motions of the textbook.

Also a rule follower, DeeDee persisted in teaching from a textbook that she believed shortchanged students. She carved out time in her schedule to offer students an inquiry approach to math. She tempered her distress about using the textbook by creating another time of the day to teach math as she believed it should be experienced. Under the cover provided by her identity as a rule follower, DeeDee created freedom as a recluse.

Acting in the role of rebel entailed that Gavin forge alliances in his school. These alliances enabled him to make changes at his own school while taking a public stand in response to city, state, and federal policies. Collaborating with other teachers enabled Gavin to be a rule changer when it came to desegregating his special education class. Likewise, his very public defiance of high-stakes testing, alongside the same stance of his coworkers, eased the way for others in the city to take on the role of rebel.

Whether recluses, rule followers, rule changers, or rebels, these teachers are disturbed by how their work, intended to be good work, negatively impacts students. They share the common moral concern that what they are expected to do as part of their professional duties conflicts with the professional commitments that motivate them as educators. They feel as though their professional moral centers are compromised and need to be righted. When teachers cannot resolve moral dilemmas posed by their work, demoralization is likely.

NAMED AS AGENTS OF HARM

This chapter begins with the premise that most teachers enter the profession because they want to contribute positively to the lives of children. The teachers described earlier in this chapter were troubled, and may have experienced demoralization, when they believed that fulfilling their professional duties caused harm to students.

Another key source of demoralization occurs when teachers are *accused* of harming students. With over twenty-three years in the same urban district, Carla's days still involved clocking long hours and weekends at the school. For over fifteen years, Monica had worked in the same suburban middle school in a nationally recognized district where she lived with her spouse and school-aged children who attended public schools. Carla and Monica each had experiences of being accused of harming students that upended their moral centers. Teachers with long records of innovation and dedication, they were alarmed and disheartened that their professional reputations were disregarded when faced with allegations of misconduct.

The experience of being accused of harming students in their care was devastating. Carla and Monica's recollections of these events take place against the backdrop of very difficult years with challenging groups of students. Each felt unsupported and alone in the months prior to and during the allegations. In their accounts, the isolation they experienced throughout the year was amplified and became intolerable when they were singled out for abusing students.

Faith offers direction and purpose in Carla's work. She has spent her entire twenty-three-year career working in a two-mile area of a Midwestern central city that has become increasingly racked by poverty and hypersegregation after busing was abandoned in the 1990s. Although she did not always envision going into teaching, she took on the work as her mission. "I knew that my mission wasn't going to be easy, and I knew that, and at times I would, I would feel very frustrated or feel like I had no control, but ultimately, I'm being called to do something. That's pretty much the way I looked at my whole career, but every missionary gets a furlough." Carla's professional moral center is informed by her religious commitments, but she did not describe her students as individuals needing to be saved by a teacher or religion. It is Carla's faith practice that keeps her centered and present in the work.

Carla describes herself as "the sort of teacher that will jump into any job that they need done." When a budget crisis left her school with no teachers to offer specials, she organized her grade-level team and developed a rotation schedule that would allow all students to have music, movement, and art every week. She'll step in to conduct choirs for special events and give presentations to the entire staff when new initiatives are rolled out.

In the year before we met, Carla felt totally depleted. She attempted to transfer to the other side of town where there was less segregation and poverty. In seeking an elementary teaching assignment in a different part of the city that would be less demanding, she did so as much for herself as for her students. She knew that she was having trouble connecting with them and that they deserved more than she was able to offer at that time.

She warned me that she might cry when we start thinking about those last years, and she does. Although she had always been strong in the area of classroom management, she was overwhelmed by the needs and behaviors of the students in her new class. In her state, teachers may be excessed, or laid off from the school, after the official student count. The principal and her colleagues were confident that Carla would succeed in taking over a fifth-grade class whose teacher was excessed. "They were all very encouraging. 'Carla, you've handled this before. We know you'd be really good in fifth grade. You're so strong.' I had a hard time saying no."

In assuming responsibility for the fifth grade mid-year, Carla encountered a class with no norms or community established. She persevered. Even though students would still occasionally tell her to "f-off" and "rip each other's hair," she could bring their behavior up to expectations so they could begin attending schoolwide assemblies. "That was the first time I felt I had no control over kids; that I couldn't teach." Even though she asked to not be placed in fifth grade the following year, she was assigned a fifth-grade class. She decided to take her chances and transfer voluntarily to another school.

Again, Carla took over a class after the start of the school year. This time, the school had too many students, and teachers were removing students off their rosters to develop a new first-grade class. Without bitterness, she explains, "As much as you don't try to dump on the new teacher coming in, my class was loaded. I had kids stabbing each other with pencils. I had kids running out of the room, and they really didn't have a classroom for me. They put me in a long rectangular computer room. I had two doorways. I had windows all around me. I felt like I was in a fishbowl."

In a new school, with a new principal, with a new class that she took over later in the year, it was the first time in Carla's career that she was given a written warning about her attitude. "I didn't disagree with the letter. Hang on," Carla wipes her tears away and gathers herself. "It was more the disappointment in myself for having become a teacher I didn't like."

A few years later, teaching third grade in the same school, Carla was overwhelmed by the behavior challenges in her class. She felt unsupported and undermined by the school's disciplinary procedures. She had initiated a restorative justice process with the class in which they would meet weekly with a local restorative justice provider and school social workers. Due to the students' behavior, the community partner and social workers agreed that the weekly meetings should be abandoned.

Against this backdrop, Carla describes a "devastating" meeting with her principal. She was summoned to the principal's office while her students were in gym. At this meeting, the principal confronted Carla with the comment, "Maybe this school isn't for you." Carla cried in shock, *anger, and frustration as a result of the accusation that challenged her dedication and effort. Likewise, she was absolutely flummoxed that the principal would drop this on her in the middle of the school day, minutes before she had to pick up her students from gym.*

In her final evaluation for the year, Carla was cited for speaking disrespectfully to the students. Although she had an opportunity to write a rebuttal, she opted to let the evaluation stand. "I just accepted it the way it was because, in my mind, I was not being the respectful person that I know I can be, but at the time, I was just getting through as best as I could."

Carla is absolutely demoralized at this point in her career. She told me that she is counting down the days until her retirement, but that isn't for another seven or eight years. She is worried that her body can't handle the work anymore. A few years ago, she hurt her shoulder breaking up a fight among her elementary school students. She doesn't physically intervene in fights anymore. She muses, "If I were looking at going into a career right now, would I choose teaching with all I know? I wouldn't."

Although the year-end evaluation and the comments from her principal sting, the most hurtful assessment is made when she compares her practice now to the teacher she has been and knows she can be. Carla wants to do right by students. When she describes students' out-of-bounds behavior, she attributes their actions to unmet needs as well as policies and practices that cluster students who struggle. Many of these contextual factors are outside of Carla's locus of control. Nevertheless, she is devastated when she looks at herself from the perspective of her professional moral center. In chapter 8, I will describe the transformation that leads Carla back to being the kind of teacher she admires and a healthier person in love with life.

Monica, a middle school teacher in an elite suburb of a major city in the Mid-Atlantic, was likewise struggling with student behavior. She was a member of a thematically focused program that faced increasing scrutiny. After her first few years working in her own subject area, she was energized by the cross-disciplinary focus and ability to team with another teacher. During the program's inception, the long-term principal gave Monica and her partner the freedom to design, recruit, and enroll students in the program. Together, they were reflective and always looking to modify or improve on their offerings.

When she thinks about why she teaches, Monica describes her purposes in moral terms. Her moral center honors the particularity of individuals who make up communities. "Ideally, [good teaching is] finding what's good in every student and, I don't know if I live up to this, helping draw that out and helping them see that. Helping students recognize their own interests and follow those. Helping them see the value, to value, the diversity that is right here. And to learn how to be part of a community." Monica is particularly cognizant of the function of ideals in teaching. She recognizes that although she may not meet her ideal, the ideal is necessary to direct her purpose.

It is easy for Monica to provide a list of the district's privileges, for students and for teachers. The community supports public education and shows that support through financial and personal investments. Families are engaged in their children's school lives and can be present for special events as well as individual conferences. Many teachers, like Monica, hold advanced degrees, although Monica is unique because she earned her PhD at an Ivy League institution prior to determining that secondary school teaching was how she wanted to spend her career. In this community, teachers are very well compensated and usually given a lot of autonomy when it comes to curriculum and pedagogy.

However, the district has also been challenged to ensure equity for all students, having been scrutinized as a result of a lawsuit in which families of lower-income black students alleged discrimination in accessing all educational programs. District personnel were on tenterhooks and had grown vigilant as a result of the case. Where the program teachers once were able to select interested students, that discretion was removed in the interest of racial and socioeconomic equity. Monica worried that not being able to be selective in enrollment could lead to students who were less invested in the program. Serving previously disenfranchised students best, she believes, entails creating engaging curriculum where their voices matter.

Over the years, Monica had witnessed long-term leadership shift, and she perceived that the district's current priorities were short-sighted and misapplied. Monica did not respect her new principal. She described him as a "weak leader" who had little classroom experience. Compared to her first principal who had been a longtime teacher and who would "say 'yes' or 'no' and why," Monica perceived this new principal as easily cowed and lacking an intellectual backbone. She had asked him several times to intervene on a "toxic combination" of students in her class that constantly disrupted lessons, but he offered little by way of advice or support.

One member of the toxic duo was Ahmad, an African American boy. Given that the chemistry of the class was challenging that year, Monica solicited letters of feedback from her students to suggest ways they could function better as a learning community. Ahmad wrote that the special program "sucked" and that he wanted out. Monica conveyed that information to the principal who said that Ahmad had to stay despite his desire to exit.

As Monica begins to recount the accusations she faced in her thirteenth year teaching, she tells me that "it was so disturbing that it sent me into an anxiety tailspin that had me going to the psychiatrist and going to therapy." Two years ago, during the principal's first year in the school and in the role, he called Monica into his office on Monday morning where she found the two assistant principals as well. She had no idea why she was there. When the principal asked if she would like a union representative present, Monica knew that whatever was going to be discussed would be serious.

The union representative arrived, who happened to be Monica's partner in the special program, and whispered, "Holy shit!" The principal thumbed through his notebook and began asking Monica questions. Soon the reason for the meeting became apparent. Monica recalls, "He was asking me if I had physically hurt children!" Apparently, Ahmad's parents had come into school and reported that Monica had put her hands on their child and hurt him. The principal turned to Monica and asked, "Did you?"

Her mind raced through countless, and honestly, difficult encounters with Ahmad. The principal became more specific, "Did you put your hand on his chin and turn his head, like this, and hurt his neck?" Monica thought, "Oh my God! There was a time in class where I was so frustrated that he was refusing to pay attention and he was such a distraction to everyone else. I put my hand on his chin and I moved his head to be facing in the right direction."

The principal then asked Monica if she had grabbed the arm of another student (the other member of the toxic duo) while on a field trip. She recalled aloud that she had given his arm a light squeeze because he was distracting others, and she was trying to wordlessly indicate that he should move to another location. Finally, he asked if Monica had broken up a fight, which she had not. Yet, she wondered, why wouldn't I do that?

"I was sitting in this room with three principals and crying. They told me that they didn't want to have this conversation on a Friday *and ruin my weekend." After the questioning, Monica asked what the next steps would be to no response. She now had to face her class, not knowing if she would be disciplined, fired, or publicly humiliated. Moments thereafter, the three principals entered Monica's classroom. The principal pulled up a chair alongside Monica, clearly taking a new tack in this encounter, and assured her that no disciplinary action would be taken. Monica asked what part race played in this situation, since she is a white woman and the student, a black boy. The principal responded that race "never occurred to him." Later in the day, the principal sought her out and inquired how she was doing.*

Monica describes this scenario as a traumatic event in her professional life. At least three different concerns may contribute to the trauma. The first is being profoundly isolated and misrecognized as a teacher. She wonders: How could my principal think that I would hurt kids? Why are the principals asking me about student discipline now when I've been requesting assistance all year? Why is it only at the point where grave lapses in professional conduct were suspected that she was engaged in any substantive conversation about the difficulties she was experiencing in her classroom?

With a thirteen-year career hanging in the balance, Monica's lack of confidence in her school leader heightened her anxiety. The stakes were high but were treated flippantly. She took the accusations seriously and wondered about the impact of the district's racial history as well as interpersonal race dynamics. This serious—and pertinent—inquiry was dismissed and rendered irrelevant.

Finally, the trauma stems from the apparent lack of regard for the moral and professional regard for teaching. A third teacher, Edwin, was accused of inappropriate behavior. However, he knew that the claim was baseless. Nonetheless, he was disturbed by how unprofessionally his principal handled a situation that could be a career-ending event.

Like Monica and Carla, Edwin was accused of harming students. A student who had already been reprimanded for spraying a teacher with a fire extinguisher had his phone out in class. Edwin walked toward the student's desk, so as not to have to yell across the room, and asked him to put away his phone. The student blurted, "Get your dick off me!" Before the end of the day, the principal was screaming at Edwin, in front of his class, demanding to know if he had made a "lewd gesture" toward a student. It was only when a student later approached the principal and told her that Edwin was being polite by walking toward the accusing student and did nothing wrong that he was exonerated. However, forget about an apology for berating him in front of his class.

Both Monica and Carla were called into their principals' offices to face serious accusations and criticisms about the harm that they allegedly inflicted on students. Their principals thought nothing of sending them back to face their students. Edwin was not given the courtesy of a private conversation. Each of the teachers recognized that any accusation made by a student needs to be taken seriously, but they were aghast that decades-long careers generated no sense of respect. All three wondered if they are romantic, old-fashioned, or just anachronistic to still hold their profession and its attendant responsibilities in such high regard.

In the next chapter, I examine the experiences of teachers who have moral concerns stemming from their participation in the degradation of teaching. They believe that practitioners have a responsibility to maintain the dignity, integrity, and worth of the profession. Their shame emerges when they realize that they have failed to uphold their vision of what teaching should be.

Some situations that teachers describe as demoralizing in terms of harm to students include:

- failing to meet students' learning needs due to a scripted curriculum or mandated textbook
- proctoring a student with cerebral palsy on a computer-based high-stakes assessment that is excruciatingly slow to complete
- following school practices that increasingly focus on academic achievement, even though students arrive at school with profound emotional needs
- witnessing students feel worthless as schools are ranked and closed
- requiring professional development that makes teachers chronically absent
- standing by as a principal intimidates students regarding their test performance
- witnessing the most vulnerable students receive the fewest resources and most pressure

CHAPTER FOUR

"I'm Admitting to Being Disingenuous in My Craft"

SOURCES OF DEMORALIZATION: DEGRADING THE PROFESSION

Gina walks with a cane and settles herself gingerly into an antigravity chair. Her two young children run around her, animated by the presence of my daughter. I worry that Gina will be jostled as the three begin a game of chase. "This," she grimaces, "is what being Teacher of the Year gets you." Gina is at the end of a year of disability leave and eyes returning to her classroom with a mixture of sadness and trepidation.

Months ago, Gina felt like a fraud as she faced her colleagues from the podium where she received her district's teacher of the year award. She had become ashamed of her work in the last several of her seventeen years teaching because of the dumbing down of teaching, the unrelenting negative press about her beloved profession, and the inequitable practices of her district. As she spoke to the eight-hundred-plus teachers, administrators, and staff members who filled the auditorium, she hoped to elevate the profession and help her colleagues feel recognized for the fine work they do each day.

As someone who finds pleasure in thinking through the challenges of teaching and learning, Gina loved that the profession called for ongoing reflection that could lead to renewed action. Gina typically enjoyed being observed because it could lead to professional conversations and growth. She recalls, "It always felt great to have another pair of eyes. I always had a great conversation afterward." She was energized by the prospects of the state's new peer-review system that had been developed in collaboration with her union. Yet, Gina was concerned with the terms that would be used to rate teachers: highly effective, effective, developing, or ineffective. "In a learning environment," Gina argues, "all of us should be 'developing.'"

The teaching standards referenced in the peer reviews were non-controversial, from Gina's perspective. The problem rested in the use of standards as a means to deliver an evaluation. She believes that the standards and the assessment process should be a starting point for serious professional conversations. She views the standards as opportunities to stimulate "some really meaty conversations about how we teach. What does student engagement look like? What does it really mean to have cognitive engagement? Does it look like them really focused? And what does focused mean?"

However, the attention to ratings suggested an evaluation system that could make individual teachers' ratings public to the school and the community. This had happened in places like Los Angeles. Also, tying the ratings to merit pay subverted an opportunity for peer-driven professional learning. Gina explains, "The teachers I know who I most respect and connect with are learners. None of this is about learning.

By attaching this process to fear, this [evaluation method] took away all potential for learning."

Instead of being engaged in meaningful conversations about teaching and learning, Gina found herself isolated in front of a computer. "I spent so much time proving that I was teaching, it left no room for teaching." She describes the paperwork associated with the assessment process as "excruciating and obscene." She says she stopped counting when she had reached fourteen hours developing materials in preparation for her observation. Gina reflects on her experience and those of the teachers she respects. Education reforms aimed at teacher accountability, she believes, didn't affect the scofflaws. "The teachers who don't care weren't made to care because of [these accountability efforts]. They just bullshit differently now. The people who were really damaged were the people who were already invested and caring and dedicated." In the midst of school budget cuts, Gina describes a systematic chipping away of morale and support because her colleagues left the school, district, and profession.

Articulating student learning objectives (or outcomes, in some states) (SLOs) proved to be one of the most time-consuming aspects of the assessment process. Gina scoured student records trying to anticipate the projected learning outcomes she could expect for students whom she had yet to meet. "I had to come home and use these tests where all of [the students] failed and figure out how to predict how many would pass in June. My husband said, 'You're crying again.' I care about teaching, and I felt like this was part of teaching. And I was literally crying every night for a month, a full month. As this district and the school and the state figured out what these things were meaning, they kept changing it. They kept saying, 'Oh, no, it actually means this. . .' And then it turned out to be a total BS phrase that we were all supposed to copy from each other that basically said 60 percent of my kids will get a 65 or above. . ."

Gina admits that she battles a perfectionist tendency, but she also believes the stakes were higher due to her public recognition. As her district's teacher of the year the same year that the new ratings were established, she understood that she would be under special scrutiny. She not only believed her work needed to be of the highest quality but also felt that her teaching now took place in a fishbowl. Now, everyone could review her ability to meet her stated student learning objectives and determine if she truly deserved the honor of teacher of the year.

Articulating the SLOs, preparing for her evaluations, and maintaining her high standards for her classroom teaching left Gina with no time to properly care for herself. Gina devoted whatever additional time she could to family. As a result, she did not exercise regularly. For many, this situation might simply lead to putting on a few pounds or not having a productive outlet for stress. For Gina, this meant that a chronic tissue disease resurfaced that left her in excruciating pain.

The avalanche of new paperwork was borne out of her state's adoption of the Common Core State Standards as well as a new assessment system. Documentation associated with professional assessments intensified without seeming to offer commensurate professional learning. More than a mere distraction, Gina felt that the so-called professional development associated with these efforts compromised the quality of her teaching. She was left with little energy to dedicate to what she loved most—engaging students with literature and helping them express themselves through writing. She was left demoralized and disabled by the effort she felt was required to be evaluated as "highly effective" and live up to her teacher of the year status.

"I wish [former US Secretary of Education] Arne Duncan would come to my living room," sighs Gina. "I don't think I wasn't who they wanted me to be. I think I was the teacher they would've wanted, you know? And yet, they broke me."

I previously examined teachers' experiences with demoralization that arose from their sense of complicity in harming students. These were "norms of client commitment" (What do students, their caregivers, and the school community deserve?). Gina, and others included in this chapter, also experienced these types of concerns. Gina's description of professional learning highlights the importance of the intellectual work for her professional moral center. Her concern for student learning and well-being fuel her intellectual interests about teaching. Gina reveals that she was thinking of leaving public school teaching. "I cannot be a part of a system that is damaging children anymore."

However, Gina also expresses serious concerns about the damage she is doing the teaching profession. For many teachers, dissatisfaction rooted in the condition and status of the profession is inseparable from concerns about students. This chapter highlights the demoralization that occurs when teachers believe that they are harming the profession that they were once proud to be a part of. These are what Lortie calls "norms of craft" (What does good teaching entail? What do my colleagues and I deserve as professionals?).[1] Most teachers experiencing demoralization feel a combination of concern for their students and their profession. Nevertheless, distinguishing these student- and professional-based facets of demoralization can result in developing distinctive and multiple approaches to re-moralizing teaching.

In a social and political climate that often interprets teachers' concerns as grievances and gripes, it is necessary to reframe the moral dimensions of teachers' work in terms of caring for the integrity of a profession, not simply caring for students.[2] Caring for the integrity of a profession entails protecting it from degradation and maintaining its boundaries that enable the profession to be recognizable as teaching. There is a subtle difference in these types of concerns. Caring for students involves asking general and specific questions such as "How does x affect all students? How does x affect Miriam, my student in third period? How does x affect Miriam, my student in third period, today?" The thorniest ethical questions emerge from context-rich situations.[3] The fact that the answers to each of these questions may be different is not the result of relativism, but a deep awareness of how context matters. What Miriam needs is not always identical with claims we would make about "all students." What Miriam needs on Monday is not necessarily what Miriam needs on Thursday.

Caring for the integrity of the profession shifts the focus to teaching. For instance, "What does it mean to engage in good teaching? What are the responsibilities of teaching? What does it mean to engage in good teaching with Miriam? What does it mean to engage in good teaching with Miriam, my student in third period, today?" While the answers to these questions may not remain constant, we can be sure that teachers are able to articulate when they have failed to uphold good teaching and when they have entered territory that they would describe as something other than teaching entirely.

CARING FOR THE INTEGRITY OF TEACHING

Caring for the integrity of teaching is a form of professional ethics. It entails a different set of questions that invite teachers to reflect on their work as professionals. These questions include, "Would other teachers I respect consider my actions good teaching? Am I engaging in conduct that honors the ideals and purposes of the profession? If others emulated my behavior, would the profession benefit?"

Many teachers may think of professional ethics as making the right decision when faced with a time-sensitive moral dilemma that calls for a response to determine the proper course of action. For instance, should Gavin have intervened during a state-mandated test when students began crying and calling themselves "dummyheads"?

Ethical decision making may occur with colleagues: should DeeDee have spoken up and told her colleagues that she believed they were selecting the lesser of the math textbooks?

Most instances of moral decision making are more quotidian. Some are also time sensitive and require an immediate response: Should I let Amir go to the bathroom? Do I need to call on a girl after hearing three boys' voices in a row? Teachers make these decisions multiple times every day of their work. Yet, they are moral because they convey messages about value. They also require a teacher's judgment. There is no rule to follow that will ensure the right answer. Sometimes, respecting Amir will be to let him know with a quick signal that he should use the bathroom. Sometimes, it is reminding Amir privately that he asks to use the bathroom each time he becomes frustrated. In this case, respect might mean helping Amir develop new tools to manage his frustration.

Other aspects of moral decision making are also built into the scope of many teachers' work but may allow for more planning and reflection. When designing lessons, teachers convey values about the kind of learning, the scope of topics, and the forms of participation they deem worthwhile. When establishing classroom norms, teachers send students messages about the ownership of the space they inhabit, the purposes of their time together, and the ways in which they should relate to each other.

Caring for the integrity of the profession involves embodying the ideals and purposes of the profession. This broadest form of professional ethics surfaces when teachers feel that they are contributing to a worthwhile form of good work. While it will take into account moral decision making, this form of professional ethics refers to teachers' holistic appraisals of their work. Do the teachers view their own embodiment of the profession as worthy of the profession?

Demoralization occurs when teachers evaluate their practice holistically and find that they are consistently moving away from the ideals and principles that they associate with the work. In these cases, they may believe that they are "giving teaching a bad name." These practitioners may believe that they are nominally teachers due to their employment and assigned role in a school. However, they would not call what they are doing teaching, in the sense of upholding the ideals of what it means to be an educator.

Gina's questions about what it takes to be recognized as exemplary highlight her holistic assessment of the state of the profession and her contributions to its degradation. As a well-prepared, driven, experienced, and passionate teacher, she was able to meet the metrics that garnered professional accolades. However, she recognized that the cost was not only her health. She believed she compromised the teaching profession by promoting an image of success that was unattainable, undesirable, and hollow.

For several consecutive years, Gina spent increasing amounts of time on initiatives promoted as professional learning, but that she found subverted the principle of ongoing professional growth and reflection. Furthermore, Gina realized that she contributed to unhealthy popular depictions of the teaching profession. She criticized the unrealistic demands on teachers and her own self-sacrifice to demonstrate excellence and commitment. Individuals in any profession may go to extraordinary lengths in the name of their work. However, Gina regretted, personally and professionally, that she propagated the teacher-as-martyr image. She posed these questions ironically: "Is this what it looks like to be teacher of the year?" and "Is this what it takes to be 'highly effective'?"

RECEIVING THE PROFESSIONAL JUDGMENT THAT STINGS

This chapter begins with Gina's demoralization in the face of degrading the profession because it might seem, to many, that she has done nothing wrong. Her experience highlights the overall assessment that takes place when teachers believe that they are giving the profession a bad name without engaging in behavior that involves students directly or that breaks specific rules or standards for teacher conduct. Nonetheless, Gina felt as though she had undermined the integrity of teaching as a profession by fulfilling all the mandates for teachers in her state, district, and building.

It is difficult to maintain a commitment to work that is historically underpaid as well as emotionally and intellectually demanding when outsiders seem to undervalue or denigrate it. Sometimes, teachers experience an inner judgment about their performance that reveals the value they place on the profession. More than simply an inner critic that issues the incessant reminder, "You could do better," the internal critique that Gina faced was that she was participating in the degradation of the profession itself. Worse than an outsider passing judgment on the poor condition of teaching is the practitioner who implicates himself or herself as a cause for that condition.

Philosopher of education Thomas Green has called this critical practitioner assessment "craft conscience." Statements of craft conscience can be accessed by reading teachers' resignation letters.[4] When teachers make claims such as "I'm no longer teaching," they do not mean that they have left the building or that they are sitting at their desks with their heads down. Instead, they are indicating that by following the rules and expectations of their *jobs*, they are degrading their *profession*. Demoralization that comes about by following the rules can occur because teaching is not identical with being employed in the role of a teacher.

When craft conscience is activated, it is

the rootedness of that voice in membership that gives the judgment its sting. That judgment hurts because it comes to us as the voice of an insider, speaking out of a shared memory and turning it against us to reveal how great a distance there is between the ideals we espouse and the realities into which, willy-nilly, we always seem to lapse.[5]

When teachers feel complicit in the degradation of the profession, they do not express remorse about failing to meet the expectations set by policy makers or disappointing their school leaders. Instead, they speak of failing to uphold the idea of good work that attracted them to teaching. They imagine the voice of the person engaged in the kind of teaching they admire, and that is what is shameful.

FAILING THE PROFESSION BY FOLLOWING THE RULES

Helen entered teaching thirty-five years ago because she found child development fascinating. As an artist, she discovered that she could satisfy her need to create and support herself through teaching. "I love using art as a tool for helping beings grow, learn, and figure out the world." Her experiences are wide-ranging—from teaching special education in New York City to working as a full-time professor of art in a rural branch of a state university to gifted education. Her passion is for teaching elementary school art.

After all this time, Helen still loves teaching. When she had a child, she took some time off but returned to the classroom inspired by her self-initiated study of Reggio Emilia. Her Reggio interest connects her with a community beyond her rural school. She joined a listserv, started a local study group, regularly attends conferences across the United States, and finally traveled to Reggio Emilia about a decade ago. The Reggio philosophy of teacher as researcher appeals to her, and she was "blown away by what they were doing with young children through the arts to bring out their expressive potential."

Teaching remains a vital and compelling interest for Helen because she continues to be enthralled by studying children as learners. By ob-

serving them and her responses to the environments she builds for them to create and learn, she feels confident in the quality of teaching she offers. "The affirmations that I get from children remind me of how important it is to stay true to the [Reggio] values." She has also built a professional community that is committed to investigating how they can promote student empowerment in the art room that enables young children to work as artists.

During our conversation, Helen peppers her commentary with research from Harvard's Project Zero and books by Diane Ravitch, and she discusses her advocacy with the state-level arts education association. Nothing about her confirms the popular image of life-long teachers as out-of-touch, ineffective, and beleaguered. Instead, her vitality has me taking notes frantically as I try to keep track of her scholarly references and activist work. She recounts studies on the effects of arts education on student achievement: that it enables them to develop capacities of experimentation and risk and cultivates the qualities of concentration and attention. "I feel very intellectually, spiritually, and creatively alive in this stage of my life, and I really love learning about how kids learn."

Giving students the opportunity to engage with art is a matter of equity for Helen. She worked on the development of learning standards for art education in her state. Given that art teachers were part of the standards development, she felt confident that they would be developmentally appropriate for children and true to the purposes of art. Her uneasiness surfaced when state leaders in art education clamored to be taken as seriously as other subjects and began agreeing to testing standards in order to confirm art's value. "They started selling off the authenticity of art education, and that for me was one of the biggest betrayals."

Standardization began to transform her building colleagues' lessons. No longer able to collaborate on project-based curricula, Helen became increasingly isolated. Colleagues resent that she still has a degree of freedom while they move to more scripted teaching. Everywhere in her rural public school, Helen feels the devaluation of art. She is excluded from IEP meetings where she used to have an important voice. She is not invited to grade-level team meetings. Her principal assumed that she can close the art room regularly, and not teach her classes, in order to allow other teachers to have prep periods. Helen is dismayed thinking of the quality of art education that children in elite private schools receive compared to that of her students.

During our interview, Helen tells me that she will leave teaching before she has to administer a state- or district-designed test to assess her students' learning. Fewer than ten months later, Helen sheepishly admits that she relented even though she said that doing so would be "not ethically teaching art to children." This is her shame. Helen believes that what she is being asked to do violates what her role should be as a teacher. "There's too much emphasis on data and proving levels and not enough on creating a culture of learning."

Helen sighs, "I'm counting the years to retirement now, in a way I never did before." Learning, as she understands it, is no longer valued in her school. She views her colleagues who unquestioningly go along with any initiative as technicians who are not living up to their professional responsibilities. Helen believes that professionals should question authority, asking "Why do we need to do this?" She is dismayed that her coworkers do not participate in local and national conversations about teaching. "I'm an intellectual, and that's hard to be in a school."

Helen possesses a sophisticated and well-articulated vision of teaching as a profession. She views investigating one's own practice as essential to responsible work. Teachers, she believes, must engage in inquiry and reflection about their students' learning and the principles that shape their planning. These investigations, Helen has realized, prove more fruitful if undertaken with thoughtful colleagues.

Increasingly alienated from the colleagues in her building, Helen found the intellectual dimensions of her professional self atrophying at school. Unfortunately, her engagement with other educators interested in thinking about student and teacher learning amplified the distance between her vision of good teaching and the priorities of standardized, rather than standards-based, learning that her school leader emphasized.

By *following* the rules of her school, by administering the pre- and post-test for her art classes, Helen committed the transgression that she had vowed not to do. Helen's demoralization can be understood as her own disappointment in what her practice has become. Being a good employee, someone who abided by the dictates of her superiors, conflicted with Helen's understanding of what it meant to be a good teacher.

Helen rarely took the silent approach that she criticized in her colleagues. Likely, the relatively young principal viewed Helen as an irritation to be tolerated and a liability to be managed. Where the school leader may have seen only insubordination or stubbornness, Helen probably interpreted her questioning as a fulfillment of her professional responsibility.

Institutions threaten to corrupt or pervert professions, according to philosopher Alasdair MacIntyre.[6] The role of practitioners is to uphold the integrity of the profession in the face of challenges to its purposes and values. Compromises will be inevitably necessary. The question will be, How far can a profession bend and still be called the same profession? For instance, Helen questioned how standardized art education could become and remain art education. For Edwin, whose experience follows, it explains how following thinly veiled demands from his supervisors "cheapens everything that I do."

Although Edwin thought he would be a college professor of Latin American and Puerto Rican Studies because of the intellectual challenge, he became more interested in working with high school students because of their energy and authenticity. He has worked at a large New York City comprehensive high school serving a majority immigrant population for eleven years. While his subject is history, he has also taught special education. Edwin also works at an evening program that supports students who have fallen behind in their studies.

In possession of two master's degrees and multiple leadership certifications, Edwin hopes to find a position where he can exert more influence in his school. "I've been kind of the utility guy. You could put me in anything and I'll do it. I volunteer for coverages. When teachers are absent, I'll sub their class. You want me to, I'll watch the suspension room." However, without connections in the Department of Education, Edwin feels that he's been at a disadvantage when applying for leadership positions. He would really like to participate in planning the master schedule.

Under his former principal, Edwin had applied for a leadership position in the school. The principal did not speak to him about his application. While Edwin sees the person who was awarded the position as extremely capable and worthy of the role, he's disappointed that he was not extended the common courtesy of acknowledgment. That principal retired last year, and with a new school leader, Edwin is more hopeful that he will be better utilized.

Given focused attention on school-level statistics, Edwin finds himself frequently asked to undermine his professionalism when it comes to passing students. When he teaches a class for seniors, he is under substantial pressure. These pressures come from individual students who have attended no more than thirty days of school; they walk in the last day of the year saying, "You will pass me." The pressures also come from principals who advocate on behalf of individual students and who ask teachers like Edwin to be mindful of publicly available statistics and their consequences.

> There was a girl who did nothing. Did absolutely nothing. Showed up late, did zero. And the principal stops me one day and said, 'Look, I know so and so failed your class, but she really needs to graduate. And all she needs is your class and two other classes to graduate. Could you change her grade? You know, I don't want to pressure you.' But, come on! You're my boss. This is the way I've kept my job. When they've given me shit, I've eaten it. And so she tells me, 'Oh, you know, I don't want to tell you . . . I just want you to look into your heart.' I'm not born yesterday. I know what that means, so I passed the kid.

It's issues of equity that get to Edwin when principals advocate for specific students. He relates another instance when he was pressured to pass a student who was chronically absent but still seen on school grounds. The student had been accepted into college and was slated to play on the football team. The school leaders stated that they were worried about how it would look to not graduate a student whose house had been destroyed by Hurricane Sandy. For Edwin, the logic didn't add up:

> You know, the student reminded me of the Zach Morris type [from television's Saved by the Bell]. He was cool, good-looking, and he was able to socialize with adults, you know. That sort of kid who could schmooze with adults. I told them that it's not fair to go to bat for him when I have some kids from Uzbekistan . . . if you guys would put some of that effort in with these kids from Uzbekistan, who put in tons of effort, but who have trouble passing the Regents Exams, these kids would graduate.

Edwin tells me he cringes when recounting all of this gaming of the system. This is his shame. "It cheapens everything I do." To balance the scales of justice, a girl who possessed none of the advantages of a Zach Morris type approached Edwin about her failing grade. He marched her *down to the guidance counselors' office and passed her. He explains, "Normally, I wouldn't have done that. I'm a pretty easy teacher."*

With the school's threat of closure looming, the pressure to pass students extends beyond the individual case to the impact on the community, the students in the school, and all those who are employed by it. Edwin isn't demoralized because he feels there is something within his control that he can do. He wants to, in his words, "quit up," and begin to address the systemic inequities that plague his school and schools everywhere. "I want to quit up because I feel like the push is more on squeezing teachers. I know they're squeezing administrators, too, but at least it'd be better to have a little more status to fend off against some of the external pressures."

Edwin's case provides an opportunity to witness the ways that school policies and mandated practices can corrupt teaching. For Edwin, violating rules and acting unprofessionally were in accordance with the directives he was receiving from his school leaders. Even when teachers like Edwin do transgress clear rules, the sense of not contributing to the good of the profession is what causes demoralization. It is the sense of undermining the integrity of what they do; in Edwin's words, it "cheapens" teaching. Rather than the fear of being caught and suffering the consequences, it is feeling as though the value of the work that gave his teaching purpose is eviscerated.

"I'M BEING DISINGENUOUS IN MY CRAFT"

Marnie's entry into teaching was deliberate and studied. After she finished high school, her parents told her that she needed to work, so she found employment as a nanny and sometimes took a class or two. In her mid-twenties, she made a commitment to finish her undergraduate degree and then landed a good job at a multinational corporation where she worked for about five years until the birth of her daughter.

Throughout the time working in the business sector, she tutored students at a credit recovery program. This experience solidified her hunch that teaching was the route to utilize her talents. Marnie possessed a purposeful sense of what she wanted out of a graduate school. She sought a teacher education program that thought about students and their communities, not just test scores. She found a school that she thought was out of her reach financially and in terms of prestige. However, she took a risk and applied for a program that offered free tuition in exchange for three years of urban teaching in the state. It was too good an opportunity to pass up just out of a lack of confidence.

The program fulfilled its promises in terms of opening opportunities to engage with the community, think deeply about the purposes and practices of teaching, and learn how to channel students' energy for learning. Marnie is entering her sixth year teaching in a small New England urban high school with over 90 percent of the majority Latinx student population qualifying for free or reduced lunch. The school was reconstituted the year before Marnie was hired, and it has yet to establish a level of stability. Much of the academic staff has turned over. Three teachers in her department left last year. Marnie and I met in the second week of August, and she still did not know what grades she would be teaching in a few weeks.

Marnie misses the opportunities for reflection and constructive feedback on teaching that were available in her graduate program. Interested in continuing that professional learning, she proposed asking about support for new teachers during a mock interview. Her district mentors told her to avoid that question at all costs because the district wanted to hire people who were "good to go." Even so, Marnie always tells her colleagues that her door is open and that she wants to receive their feedback. "I encourage people to come in because you're going to see something that I'm not going to see. I might miss something that you see. And that, to me, is going to make me a better teacher . . . I think good teaching is acknowledging that my way isn't always going to be the best way, and I need to be open to and receptive to what others have done."

As an educator who comes with the perspective that good teachers are always learning and growing, Marnie was baffled by the evaluation procedures. As the stakes raised, components of the evaluation process ultimately became the source of her shame. Her first year, before the adoption of the Danielson framework for assessment, she was given a perfect score. "There's no way I'm a perfect teacher. I'm good, don't get me wrong. But, really? A perfect score my first year of teaching?"

The high stakes of testing at Marnie's school created tensions and compromised the integrity of assessments and the quality of relationships. In the middle of a class period, the principal called an impromptu meeting for all the sophomores in the cafeteria. Due to the school's low test scores, the principal told the students that they had to practice using an online program. He distributed contracts that he directed the students to sign, affirming that they would follow through on this additional math help. The contract, Marnie heard the principal say, needed to be signed; otherwise, he would begin paperwork to transfer the students out of the school.

Listening, Marnie thought about how she would feel if her daughter came home saying that she was asked to sign something without looking it over together. She raised her hand and said, "Just to clarify, should their parents see it before they sign it? And, if they don't sign it, they're going to be moved to a different school?" The principal denied the threat but was met with over fifty "yes-you-dids" from the teenagers in the room. In hindsight, Marnie realized that she might have handled the situation with more tact, but she was very concerned with her students' rights *being violated at that moment. She sees her role as an advocate for her students, not simply an instructor of a subject.*

Marnie believes that she was targeted for unfair treatment as a result of that interaction and other times when she asked relevant questions as an exercise of her professional responsibility She soon learned how using a teacher assessment model that is rubric-based, like Danielson's, could produce radically different results. After three years of receiving threes and fours (effective and highly effective), the principal with whom she had conflict rated her with ones and twos (ineffective and developing). The following evaluation cycle, someone else conducted the process and she was back to threes and fours.

Confident in her abilities as a teacher and now with tenure, Marnie is not terribly concerned about the numbers associated with her evaluations. Her shame arises from her dishonesty when assessing student learning outcomes now that they are associated with teacher evaluations. She shakes when she begins to tell me about her collusion with a colleague to inflate scores when scoring essays to ensure that her coworker had met student learning outcomes. Although she knows other pairs of teachers feigned "objective" scoring, too, she still finds her behavior inexcusable. Her voice quavers as she whispers, "I'm admitting to being disingenuous in my craft."

She lives in fear that someone will ask her to provide evidence to support her data. Yet, that moment has not come. As a form of self-imposed penalty, she chose not to claim that she had met 100 percent of her student learning objectives and earned the designation "effective" rather than "highly effective." Marnie felt pressured by the more experienced teacher with whom she was supposed to trade papers for scoring who refused to have anything less than 100 percent of her student learning objectives met. The teacher insisted Marnie meet with her after school and off the grounds. She had prepared all of the scoring sheets but pressed

Marnie to re-create them all in her hand. Marnie did not ask the same from her coworker. "All of this defeats the purpose of an evaluation."

Some teachers, like Marnie, believe that school policies and practices created the conditions that induced them to violate their ideals about good teaching. She found that it was nearly impossible to have an assessment process that contributed to authentic and honest professional development, even one that was rolled out as expensively as the online Danielson component. Marnie's shame is not simply about feeling guilty for wrongdoing, it is connected to questions about good teaching and if what she is doing has the value she imbues it with.

Many teachers, including Diane, who will be introduced in the next chapter, are unsure of where to turn when they believe that they are engaging in wrongdoing or believe that they are being asked to engage in illegal practices. Diane, after taking a stand against the role of standardized testing in her school, was told by her union that she was on her own.

It is not obvious if many of the kinds of concerns raised by these teachers would meet the criteria for whistleblower protections. The most clearly articulated whistleblower provisions exist at the state level, but not all states offer these sorts of protections. Federal law is muddier. Supreme Court cases such as *Lane v. Franks* (2014) and *Garcetti v. Ceballos* (2006) have not offered conclusive descriptions of the conditions that need to be met for public employees' speech to be protected.

In the absence of obvious and safe channels to explore professional ethical dilemmas, teachers are left to navigate these complex emotions and situations on their own. The experience of feeling isolated with these challenging dilemmas may lead to demoralization.

My exploration of the interaction between school policies and teacher behavior is not meant to excuse or justify wrongdoing. However, it does provide a backdrop and context for the violation of professional ideals and sometimes even laws. Some of the sources of demoralization teachers described in terms of degradation of the profession are:

- colluding with colleagues on grading assessments that are used to determine teacher ratings and pay
- being pressured by school leaders to pass students to improve publicly available graduation rates
- experiencing an onslaught of one-directional communication about teaching that does not include the voices of practitioners (inside and outside schools)
- witnessing school leaders' rejection of teacher expertise and initiative in favor of adopting expensive products and services that yield dubious results
- observing and undergoing threats to due process
- observing alternative and fast-track licensure programs that degrade and deprofessionalize teaching
- being assigned to sham professional learning communities that provide the illusion of teacher voice
- having school leaders who do not tell returning faculty what they are teaching until the week before students arrive
- witnessing colleagues fail to pull their weight or be unwilling to improve their practice
- witnessing colleagues leave the profession

CHAPTER FIVE

"I Can't Be That Kind of Teacher"

RE-MORALIZING STRATEGIES FOR CAREER LONGEVITY

Yesi is a first-year science teacher, but this year marks her twenty-first year teaching. About twenty minutes into our conversation, we are interrupted by a school tour. Yesi welcomes prospective families beginning the daunting process of New York City kindergarten admissions into her early elementary classroom. She describes the school garden accessible through an exterior door on the eastern wall, talks about how she meets the needs of all students by differentiating her instruction, and discusses the routines of the school day.

The parents are visibly on edge as they imagine what it would be like to send their children to a progressive public school of choice. Some want to ensure that their children will meet state-determined benchmarks for achievement. Others are concerned about English acquisition. Still others inquire how the enrollment of one child might affect the prospects of a younger sibling. Throughout all these questions, Yesi makes the parents feel *as though she has no other obligations: no interviewer crouched at a pint-sized table, no students about to burst onto the scene in fifteen minutes.*

None of the anxious parents and guardians know that Yesi's mother-in-law passed away yesterday. Aware that I was traveling especially for the opportunity to speak with her, Yesi arrived at school today ready to meet with me. I try to impress that we can find another time to talk, but she insists that we use our time together well.

This year marks the start of Yesi's science teaching and her first time working with first- and second-grade students. Because she has taught for over two decades, it would be reasonable to describe Yesi as closing in on the third act of her career. Instead, Yesi chose to begin again, despite the difficulties, to renew her love of the work.

Yesi's new position has presented novel challenges. More accustomed to working with later elementary grades, she told me that she has made her first and second graders cry unintentionally this year. She's learning to gear the material to the correct level and present students with manageable challenges that are not tear-worthy.

When she first began in the New York City public schools, in the early 1990s, Yesi was hired in a school slated "for revision," which meant it was about to be closed by the district superintendent. She recalls sitting on her desk, students rapt as she read an African story told in the oral tradition, when she was startled to attention by the principal shouting across the room, "Ms. Garcia, What are you doing? This is the 'golden reading' hour. Why aren't they all reading?" Never mind that the textbooks that students were expected to read from during the "golden hour" were at least a quarter-century old, explains Yesi, they were "racist, noninclusive, the worst." The principal made the students get up, retrieve the textbooks from the back of the room, turn to page thirty-five, and start reading. Yesi never recovered her students' trust that year. She recalls, "I was completely usurped. Those kids were like, 'You can't protect us and we don't care about you.'"

Her strength that first year came, in part, from a group that met at a local college. She says that she would not have made it without a place to find emotional support, access teaching materials, and be reminded regularly of the progressive ideals that inspire her. Tapping back into these progressive roots is the reason that Yesi made the move to science.

Yesi had been "feeling very stale" and considered leaving the school where she has taught for the last five years. She attributed her dissatisfaction to having taught the same grades for twenty years, but also to the ways curricular practices, even in a somewhat progressive school, make it difficult to develop a curriculum that emerges from students' interests. In the past, Yesi's classes

> *studied immigration because a little girl came in and said that the newspaper guy on 190th Street was getting deported . . . We had this huge [public transportation] strike, and we started to talk about human rights and . . . what it meant to be a worker and what worker's unions were, and that's how curriculum developed. It was never the way it is now; you preplan it, and* Understanding by Design, *and backward planning . . . it's not ever coming from kids anymore.*

Yesi finds science a way to stay connected to her progressive roots. Scientific inquiry enables her students to pursue questions that come from their lives and the material under investigation.

A commitment to the ideals of the profession and high expectations for her own performance set Yesi looking for other positions. Her self-assessment: "It's good enough, but [I was] just doing the bare minimum. It's not [good enough], when you know what you can do. I can't be that kind of teacher." When a position for a science teacher opened in her current school, she leapt.

Having participated in a number of STEM-related professional de-
velopment grants at her previous school, Yesi was ready to make the
switch to science teaching. Currently, Yesi is collaborating with a team
at the same local college that offered her a space to grow her first year.
The professor/practitioner team is developing a physics curriculum for
young children based on the Next Generation Science Standards (NGSS).
Yesi is hoping to bring the team's work to the district, to the state and,
ultimately, to the national level.

Teacher resilience, whether seemingly innate or consciously cultivated, is touted widely as the answer to the problems of teacher
retention.[1] Those who promote resilience in teacher education literature present it as the silver bullet that will enable teachers to keep
teaching, against all odds. This chapter highlights the shortcom-
ings of deploying resilience as a means to address teachers' moral
sources of dissatisfaction with institutional policies and practices.
It also presents re-moralizing strategies that can help teachers take
action when their moral motivations for teaching are challenged.

Popular and scholarly calls to cultivate teacher resilience pre-
sume that teachers currently *lack* resilience. Those who suggest that
teachers lack resilience point to dismal retention figures, especially
for those in their first five years of teaching. The linkage between
poor retention and teachers' lack of resilience reflects a leap in
logic that is not borne out by the data. Current survey measures
are not sufficiently fine-grained to reveal if some attrition may be
the result of "leavers'" refusal to engage in practices and follow
policies that they perceive as damaging to students, their communities, and the teaching profession, rather than a poor ability
to rebound from challenges.

Teachers need to have personal reserves and interpersonal resources that enable them to withstand the challenges inherent to

teaching. That point is without question. However, the experience of demoralization reveals that resilience as a response to teacher retention challenges has its limits. Teachers' professional moral centers may require that they push back with resistance rather than bounce back with resilience.

Teachers may leave the profession when they are not able to resolve moral concerns about their work. They may refuse to be complicit in practices that harm students and that denigrate the practice of teaching.[2] Teachers committed to the profession often go to great lengths, as Yesi's experience shows, to resolve concerns and conflicts so they can remain in the classroom. Sometimes, teachers fiercely committed to their students and relentlessly dedicated to the profession find that they are unable to remain in the classroom when their values are continuously compromised.

ARE TEACHERS LACKING RESILIENCE?

Resilience, as it is commonly understood, calls for teachers to find balance, practice mindfulness, and reach out for emotional support. Often, resilience entails accommodating one's behavior and expectations to accept and adapt to conditions as they are. Cultivating resilience is an important achievement; my argument in no way disparages practices that enhance mindfulness or that build an individual's capacity to face life's challenges. However, as a response to demoralization, calls for resilience can be experienced as an ineffective and insulting recommendation. Diagnosing teachers as requiring a dose of resilience fails to address the institutional, systemic, and policy-based origins of a moral problem. It suggests that accommodation is always the best answer when realistically strategic resistance may be necessary.

Inundated with calls to become more resilient, teachers likely hear the message as an indictment of their supposed lack of strength.

For example, urban teaching researcher Christopher Emdin criticizes practices that call on black male teachers to enact punitive school policies that perpetuate the criminalization and devaluation of black and brown minds and bodies. When black male teachers realize that they cannot in good conscience contribute to this cycle of failure, he says, they may quit. Then, it is likely that those teachers are condemned for lacking resilience or, also popular, "grit." In Emdin's words: "The source of this often sits at the precipice of pessimists who get to spit a less legit hypothesis about my grit, when it's obvious that I am forced to fit in a system. So, I quit."[3]

Researchers, school leaders, and teacher educators need to investigate the sources of teacher dissatisfaction and attrition before leaping to recommendations to cultivate resilience. Yesi persevered through an incredibly challenging first year of teaching. She found a community of like-minded educators through a university-based mentoring program. Today, she continues to collaborate with professors and other K–12 teachers by developing curriculum aligned with the NGSS.

Yesi possesses personal and professional resilience. She met with me the day after her mother-in-law's passing, and she applied for a new position in her school to ensure that she continues to stay engaged in her work. However, Yesi continues to teach due to a degree of luck, not only resilience.

The year prior to our conversation, Yesi determined that she could not, in good conscience, administer high-stakes tests to her students. She joined a coalition of other teachers in her school to declare their conscientious objection to the tests. When Yesi refused to administer the state proficiency exams to her fifth-grade students, she was not fired, was not ostracized by faculty, and faced no retribution from her school leaders. Had Yesi faced formal or informal negative consequences and decided to leave teaching, suggesting that she should have cultivated greater resilience would have missed the mark. Instead, her problem was with the moral problems that arose in her teaching, not her ability to withstand challenges.

Consider Edwin's experience (detailed in chapter 4) as an example of personal and professional resilience. During his first teaching job, Edwin's mother succumbed to brain cancer. Edwin continued his semester of master's work at a local college but was not able to keep up the B average required to maintain his tuition funding. The next year, while he was in his second year of teaching, he transferred to another college where he had also received an acceptance. He completed his master's degree and graduated with a 3.9 grade point average.

Although Edwin had a lot to be proud of in his early years, he also faced some shameful failures. In his first few years of teaching, he received a letter of reprimand from a principal for poor teaching. Recognizing the elements of truth in this official rebuke, he redoubled his efforts and made a point to tutor students before and after school. Without his personal and professional resilience, it is highly unlikely that Edwin would be in his eleventh year of teaching.

Edwin's current dissatisfaction with his work, however, cannot be remedied with an added dose of resilience. Instead, he is worried about the ways in which he is implicated in a system that renders academic integrity meaningless. He is concerned about perpetuating practices that offer distinct advantages to the already-privileged. These are moral concerns that, left unaddressed, could lead to demoralization.

Diane has taught in the same Midwestern school district for twenty-one years. It is a district that regularly makes the list of top schools in national magazines, and Diane says that it is a place that she has, at times, described as "visionary." She has spent the majority of her career working with sixth, seventh, and eighth, grades. Recently, she took a two-year sabbatical to finish her doctorate.

Returning to her school activated Diane's moral concerns. While she was completing her degree, the district hired a full-time substitute teacher to cover her classroom. Diane believed that she would be contributing to the damage of the profession by stepping right back into her old position and displacing the substitute. "She'd done this great job, and they were just going to kick her to the curb. So, when I came back, I specifically said that I did not want that position."

Diane did not want to participate in the labor practices that made it easy to discard an employee who had been a valuable member of the school. She recalled that when she was first hired, members of the district informed her, in front of her students, that her contract was going to be terminated. Someone who had seniority was returning from sabbatical and needed a position. "It put me in the worst place possible with the kids. I had been teaching sex ed, so it was already completely silent. I can re-member turning around to shocked faces. That felt really uncomfortable."

Diane's concerns about displacing another teacher who had demon-strated commitment and success were motived by more than a desire to avoid harming others and an expression of labor solidarity. Diane's moral center includes commitments to the professional distinctiveness and responsibility of teachers. Her values direct her to resist policies that treat teachers as interchangeable, even when those policies would be to her benefit.

It would seem that Diane should be inoculated from demoralization. She was allowed a two-year sabbatical in a highly regarded district that prioritizes innovative approaches to teacher learning. She has National Board certification, multiple advanced degrees and certifications, and now, a doctorate. She has taught frequently for the district's summer professional development program. Local colleges and universities call on her to teach courses and mentor student teachers. Diane has won numerous grants that have benefitted her own classroom and the district.

Diane returned from sabbatical reflecting on her time away and her role as a teacher leader. To her mind, earning her doctorate raised the stakes for her own practice. "Getting those three little letters behind your name means something morally and ethically. At least it did to me." Diane viewed her role as exercising moral leadership by practicing her professional values publicly. This modeling also involved taking a stand against high-stakes testing.

When Diane began teaching in the mid-1990s, she recalled that teachers feared the arrival of the "proficiency police." Supposedly, the "proficiency police" would ensure that classrooms met the testing environment requirements. "Your room needs to be stripped down, everything has to be covered. You can't have any bulletin boards up. You can't have the American flag up."

Diane recalled administering her first high-stakes practice test. She had dutifully prepared her room and read from the script provided by the state. Frightened that the "proficiency police" were outside her door, Diane followed the regulations to the letter:

> So, I go to sit at my desk. We were told not to walk around. We were told not to really even make much eye contact with the kids. I had kind of prepared them that this isn't going to be a typical day. Usually, you can ask me questions anytime you want to, but you're not allowed to [during the practice or actual test]. Ten minutes go by, and Molly raises her hand. I give her the teacher look like, "How dare you raise your hand?" and she puts her hand down. Then, she tentatively puts her hand up again.

Since it was practice, Diane rationalized that she could at least let Molly know that she was not allowed to assist her. She approached her student's desk. Molly pointed as she whispered, "I don't know this word." The word was "selection" as in "Read the selection and answer the questions." Diane remembered telling her, "'I'm sorry, honey, I'm not allowed to pronounce the word for you. Do the best you can'. . . Bawling."

There is enough emotion in Diane's voice that I needed to ask who was bawling. "She was bawling. I was feeling like the worst person on the face of the earth. She could not keep it together. She asked to go to the restroom and I let her go. That evening I got a phone call from her parents. They were calling to apologize because Molly was pretty sure that I would lose my teaching license because she asked me a question. Now, never in one instance, had I mentioned the 'proficiency police.'"

More than twenty years later, the testing stakes have increased, and the exams are more frequent. After that first year, Diane was determined that she would learn everything possible about the test and prepare her students to beat it. She believed the "torturous" testing conditions could be allayed through readiness. Diane developed what she called "boot camps" where she would ensure that students like Molly were familiar with the vernacular of the tests. Because the boot camps stressed her students and were unauthentic interruptions to the school's well-planned curriculum, Diane eventually abandoned them. "I've just decided that the scores aren't going to be the thing that drives me. I performed the worst of my colleagues once I chose not to play the game." This year, Diane's colleagues agreed that the boot camps detracted from good teaching, and they all stopped engaging in intensive test preparation. The empty promises made by the test company to return student data in time to inform teachers' work have made Diane and her colleagues even less invested in the process.

With more than two decades of experience, Diane possesses a clarity of purpose that takes precedence over her desire to follow the rules. She aligns her actions with her professional beliefs rather than mandates dictated by a testing company.

As a teacher, my job is to answer questions for kids. As a teacher, it's my job to make my students feel safe and cared for and part of a community. These kids were nine years old. They have certain adults in their lives that they're supposed to be able to trust and that they care for. The fact that Molly felt that she was hurting me in any way, shape, or form by not being able to perform was wrong. It was wrong that I couldn't answer a child's question or that I couldn't read a word for her. Everything I'd been taught had already said that these are the things you're supposed to do for kids. You're supposed to help them to get to the next level. And, if you are giving them a test, it should be appropriate to what they know and are able to do. I had words and actions of things that I wanted to be as a teacher, and I was able to enact it until this point. At this point, I was no longer able to be that person that I know I want to be. I have to be this other person who feels monstrous, actually.

Diane estimated that in the last five years, she has written over two hundred letters to legislators, departments of education, and newspaper editors. Prior to Diane's taking her PhD, few recipients responded to her letters. Earlier this year, she wrote a letter telling parents about their right to opt their children out of high-stakes testing and posted it on Facebook. Her state's Badass Teachers Association reposted the letter, then the local parents' group posted it on its blog, and soon television media and national news services wanted to talk to Diane.

REBELS, RULE CHANGERS, RULE FOLLOWERS, AND RECLUSES: PART II

Teacher resilience, defined as an educator's ability to withstand difficult situations and bounce back from adversity, is prevalent in all the teacher narratives that appear in this book. Without resilience, it is unlikely that any of the teachers would have continued past their first year of teaching. Some of them, decades later, still recalled those early profession-rattling experiences. Nevertheless, they continue to teach five, ten, twenty, and thirty years later.

Resilience, however, does not immunize teachers from the threat of demoralization. Demoralization occurs when teachers believe that they are complicit in harming their students or damaging their profession. These are *moral* challenges that threaten their definition of good work. If these kinds of challenges become endemic and persistent, they may lead to demoralization.

Demoralized teachers may leave the profession that once was the source of their good work. Quitting may seem to be the only option for those who cannot find a way to resolve ongoing and persistent moral conflicts.[4] Experienced teachers who resign for moral reasons may, in fact, be demonstrating resilience by finding ways to live their values that are less fraught with conflict or contradiction. Some teachers who experience demoralization take a stand against policies and practices that they believe undermine the integrity of teaching and that cause students' harm.

Experienced teachers describe a number of actions that they took to stave off demoralization or to re-moralize their teaching practice. The strategies that contributed to their re-moralization in the face of moral challenges are more proactive and community-oriented than the kind of personal bounce-back usually invoked in the teacher resilience literature.

The strategies used by teachers to re-moralize their practice fall into five broad, and often overlapping, categories: *student-centered action, teacher leadership, activism, voice,* and *professional community,* as shown in figure 5.1. The variety of the categories enables teachers to take possibly re-moralizing action that aligns best with their professional contexts and individual dispositions.

FIGURE 5.1   Strategies for re-moralization

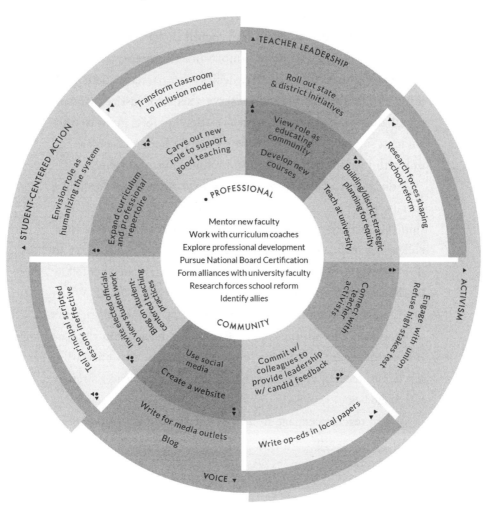

- PROFESSIONAL COMMUNITY
- VOICE/WRITING
- ACTIVISM
- TEACHER LEADERSHIP
- STUDENT-CENTERED ACTION

Student-centered action often takes place between teachers and their students. It may take the form of a shift in perspective that guides teachers' curricular and pedagogical choices, such as Diane's decision to end test-prep boot camp. Student-centered action may guide a teacher's, like Edwin's, decision to pass a student with less social capital in order to preserve a sense of justice. This re-moralizing strategy may also involve applying for a grant to offer students summer support to prepare them for honors classes, as Lee did with incoming immigrant and refugee ninth graders.

Educators engaged in *teacher leadership* do not need to hold a specific title to enact these strategies. Teachers engage in leadership that may re-moralize their practice when they involve their colleagues in practices or actions that reestablish their ability to do good work. Diane took this step when she persuaded her fellow teachers to stop using curricular time for test preparation. When Gavin advocated for his self-contained special education students to be integrated with their grade-level peers, he acted in the best interest of students (student-centered action) by demonstrating teacher leadership. Hilary deployed teacher leadership as a strategy when she began exploring ways to shift to a teacher-led school.

When teachers engage in *activism*, they take a specific public stand for or against a policy or practice. The activism may be supported by the union, as was the case with Jason (upcoming in chapter 7) when he demanded that Teach For America not receive a contract in his city that was flowing with newly certified teachers looking for work. Yesi's letter to district leadership saying that she refused to administer high-stakes tests also is a form of activism.

Voice plays a significant role in re-moralization. Many teachers attribute their demoralization to an inability to have their voice heard. Diane wrote hundreds of letters without a single response. Suddenly, her voice, in the form of a Facebook post, was amplified by the Badass Teachers Association and a local parent advocacy group.

United Opt Out validated Diane's use of voice in ways that felt essential to her at a time when she was being vilified for speaking out. Vanessa, whose experience is discussed in chapter 6, felt as though she was going mad when she criticized and questioned her district's shift in policy. She found an outlet in blogging where she quickly developed an audience that affirmed the critical lens she brought to district decision making. Voice may be spoken, written, or signed.

Professional community is positioned at the center of figure 5.1 because it is the category that permeates all others. Some aspects of this strategy involve simply being with like-minded individuals and identifying allies. Strategies for re-moralization are weakest at the outermost edges of the figure, where individuals work alone to enact a strategy. We can see this effect clearly in Diane's experience. After utilizing her voice on her own, she felt vulnerable and isolated. When she linked into the United Opt Out network, which recognized her courage, she found strength and support.

Even though Diane's professional community is strong, it was not connected to her use of voice. Professional community is also weak when not combined with another strategy. Sometimes, professional community provides the base for action, such as the partnership that Gavin established for an inclusive classroom. However, at other times, professional community may arise out of shared action in other categories. For Helen, the Reggio community across the United States and in Italy provided her with a touchstone as she enacted student-centered art education.

Teachers who have moral concerns about their work do not necessarily need to raise their voices as conscientious objectors, whether or not their conscientious objection involves quitting as a form of refusal. Some teachers do embrace the role of rebel, but others identify strongly as rule followers. Some work to change the rules through advocacy and alliances, whereas others try their best to avoid detection as recluses while they quietly teach according to their professional conscience. Even the most reclusive teachers in this study referenced *professional* values and commitments, not simply personal ones. Even though the decisions individual teachers made might not be agreed upon by others, they existed within a professional vernacular that could be recognized as a legitimate teaching option and discussed.

Even though some recluses may alter the rules and hope to continue undetected or unmolested, many teachers remarked that it was no longer possible to "just close your door and teach" due to frequent monitoring by school leaders, district and state personnel, or paid consultants. Even recluses, like Nina, usually found professional community through conferences as well as professional literature and research. Many teachers spoke of the quality of professional community that they found online that extended their possible colleagues across the United States and throughout the globe. Specific online-generated communities such as the Badass Teachers Association, the Network for Public Education, and United Opt Out not only introduced teachers to colleagues from afar but also helped them better identify nearby allies.

Figure 5.1 includes specific strategies described by the teachers in this study to offer examples of actions that rebels, rule followers, rule changers, and recluses may employ to re-moralize their work. In some situations, teachers can transform and interrupt the conditions that contributed to their demoralization. While some teachers are politically active, others avoid politics and focus on teaching and learning within their school community. Figure 5.1 is not meant to be an exhaustive list of re-moralizing actions. Instead, the specific examples within each category are presented to stimulate ideas about possible actions in different teaching contexts by teachers with distinct dispositions.

Figure 5.1 enables teachers to envision multiple points of entry and various types of re-moralizing actions. Re-moralizing action can be taken on one's own or with a well-recognized group. Action may entail the invisible—for instance, a conscious reframing of one's work—or the highly visible, such as a public protest. The strategies are represented circularly to indicate that no form of re-moralization is better or more praiseworthy than another. The strategies that teachers use to re-moralize their work will depend on their teaching context, their ability to engage in professional risk, their personality, and their personal circumstances.

Let's take Diane's experience as an example. Although Diane had always identified herself as a rule follower, she unexpectedly found herself occupying the role of rebel. As a rule follower, her first strategy to re-moralize her practice when confronted with high-stakes assessments was to "beat the test." This is an example of *student-centered action*. Diane sought to empower her students with the knowledge they would need to be prepared. She hoped that such preparation would stave off future emotional harm, such as that experienced by Molly.

Diane's *student-centered action* moved from the outer circle of the diagram to the inner when she collaborated with her team members on the testing "boot camps." Here, she enlisted her *professional community* to engage in student-centered action. When Diane later convinced her team members to abandon the boot camps due to the ways they detracted from their curriculum and added unnecessary weight to the high-stakes tests, Diane moved along the middle ring to the intersection of *student-centered action*, *teacher leadership*, and *professional community*.

The sudden media attention Diane received after her letter to parents about their opt-out rights was distributed led to her sobbing in a middle school closet. "I couldn't handle it anymore and just went in there and cried. I was so sad because I felt so alone." Due to her appearance on television news, people throughout the district began to refer to Diane as a celebrity. Her new status was even more fraught because she had returned from sabbatical with a PhD. She faced a mixture of resentment and awe in response to both her degree and her decision to take a stand. Her board of education had called her an "unruly teacher." During a faculty meeting, her principal accused her of unprofessionalism. The union's local chapter leader told Diane that she was on her own since her state did not grant teachers whistleblower status. Her union would not support her speaking out against the value of the tests and ignoring district directives to tell students and their families that they were obligated to take the tests. Her colleagues shunned her. "Most were like, 'You go! Keep going, you're doing a great job! By the way, don't sit next to me.'"

Diane learned that principals in every school building across the district were reading statements denouncing her actions as unprofessional. "I realize words have consequences," Diane explained, "but [my actions were] done out of a place of professionalism, so don't discount that." As an example of her motivations based on moral leadership, Diane let her superintendent know that a district office employee was providing families with false information about their obligation to take the test. Diane was concerned about possible legal action that the district might encounter as a result of the falsehood. Her more powerful motivation came from a place of professional ethics. Individuals in positions of power or with specialized knowledge, she believes, have the obligation to tell the truth and inform families and children of their rights. Even though the district described Diane's actions as "unprofessional," she knew that she was acting from her own professional moral responsibility.

A pariah in her district, Diane turned to her computer and contacted United Opt Out for support. The leaders of the national movement immediately recognized her on the website for her courage in defending the rights of children and their parents. "Just the fact that other people were calling me brave meant something," Diane recalls. She could also turn to this online community to hear the experiences of other teachers who had spoken out in accordance with their professional conscience. Additionally, she received practical advice about handling media inquiries.

As a science teacher, Diane would not be required to administer the proficiency exams. Nonetheless, her district wanted her to sign off on the confidentiality contract required by the test makers. Diane refused; she would not see the test anyway, so what was the point? "The principal asked, 'Are you going to be morally and ethically opposed to giving the [end-of-year subject area test]?' And I said, 'I probably am.' This is hard for me because there's this piece of me that wants to protect my kids from it. I don't want them to have to be in the room with anybody else. Since the first test [where Molly broke down], I go around, I pat them on the back. I give them words of encouragement. I try to be as supportive of them as I can, in that moment."

The principal later returned to explain that the social studies teachers would administer both the science and social studies tests that year. Diane explained that the principal's plan to avoid conflict put her in an ethical bind. "I'm not sure how to feel about that. Why are my social studies teachers having to give the test? Now, I'm thankful that [my students] will be with their teacher. . ." Diane struggled with how her commitments to avoid harming may result in her harming her colleagues and the school's professional community.

When Diane used her *voice* to address her letter to parents, she knew that she was taking a risk and that her writing was public. However, she had not anticipated the degree of public attention she would receive and the isolation she would feel in a community where she had felt strongly connected. Her use of *voice* existed first at the outer ring of the diagram. It was here that she felt most vulnerable and exposed.

When she connected with United Opt Out and was recognized for using her *voice*, she moved into the middle ring that combines *voice* with *professional community*. Her conversations with leaders from United Opt Out precipitated her decision not to give the state proficiency test in her subject area. Her strategies then moved to the intersection of *voice*, *activism*, and *professional community*.

Diane employed a number of strategies, in a variety of categories, but those actions did not guarantee that she would resolve all of her dilemmas. The strategies enabled her to feel less morally conflicted about her work in terms of harming students and denigrating the teaching profession. Yet, it is clear that these strategies did not eliminate questions about professional ethics. Strategies for re-moralization are ways that teachers, like Diane, find they can partially reconcile substantial and ongoing moral concerns about their work.

AUTHENTIC PROFESSIONAL COMMUNITY AT THE CENTER

While no one strategy promises success and no particular category in the figure is better than another, whenever strategies intersect with professional community, they seem to provide a stronger and more sustainable base from which to act. All strategies that involve professional community (everything except the outermost ring) do not depend on the singular actions of one teacher. However, at the same time, professional community itself (the hub) is usually insufficient to spark re-moralization on its own. When an individual teacher's spirit or energy flags, authentic professional community supplies other colleagues who can continue the work until the teacher is restored. This continuity combats feelings of futility and the myth that one person can do good work isolated from others. Professional community can provide support and an opportunity to share acquired wisdom. Furthermore, when teachers act with professional community, the risk that individual teachers may bear in taking action for re-moralization can be shared and potentially minimized.

The majority of the strategies that led to teachers experiencing re-moralization involved connecting with their professional community: identifying allies at their school and in their district, participating in leadership opportunities in their unions, finding education and support through participation in online activist organizations, identifying and informing parents of their shared interests and concerns through blogging, and forging partnerships with local higher education faculty. Even those strategies that seem individualized (such as committing to humanize a dehumanizing experience for students) reference an implied community of teachers who could recognize the professional and moral value of the action or approach.

Professional community appears at the center of this diagram of re-moralization strategies because it serves as the hub for all others. I define professional community as the other professionals who give meaning, purpose, and direction to teachers' work. These are the people that teachers seek out for advice, support, and collaboration. Professional community does not mean the professional learning community (PLC) a school leader might direct to meet between 2:30 and 3:15, although in fortuitous instances, this might turn out to be such a resource. Almost always, authentic professional community is *chosen* by those who make up its membership.

Vanessa, introduced in the next chapter, recalled proposing a districtwide PLC to her principal. As someone running a special program at her school, she felt that she could benefit from collaborating with others doing the same in another building. Instead, the principal insisted that she work with building colleagues. The principal-determined PLC was not conducted professionally nor did it result in learning. Although sometimes school leaders have goals that need to be met through particular group configurations, teacher-directed opportunities to collaborate may produce more significant and meaningful results.

In authentic professional communities, teachers articulate and refine their professional values and accompanying practices in conjunction with colleagues and partners who seek to do the same. The pace of instructional days and the loss of curricular and pedagogical autonomy in many schools may offer morally motivated teachers few opportunities to enact or reflect on their professional moral centers. Engaging with professional community, collaborating with a coteacher, participating in live monthly Twitter chats, or meeting regularly with a local union caucus may provide teachers with an opportunity to feel productive in their commitments to their students and their profession.

I am a teacher educator who depends on experienced teachers to offer their limited time for insufficient monetary compensation to mentor my preservice students. Analyzing these re-moralizing strategies revealed some surprises. Although teachers are experiencing intensification in their work, college, university, and community organizations should not predetermine that teachers are not interested in opportunities for collaboration. For many of the teachers I have interviewed, connections with professors and university programs contributed significantly to their professional longevity. These collaborations provided teachers who were experiencing demoralization ways to enact their moral centers that felt meaningful and impactful.

This chapter discussed the strategies that teachers can employ to try to re-moralize their work. However, some strategies are facilitated or enabled by school leaders and teacher unions. The next two chapters examine the ways that these influential groups in the professional lives of teachers may contribute to demoralization and also how they may facilitate re-moralization.

Almost all the strategies that led to teachers experiencing re-moralization involved connecting with their professional community. When teachers take action with members of their professional community, those actions seem to be the most secure, sustainable, and efficacious. Teachers can find strategies that align with their concerns, contexts, and dispositions. Some examples include:

- identifying allies at their school and in their district
- participating in leadership opportunities in their unions
- finding education and support through participation in online activist organizations
- identifying and informing parents of their shared interests and concerns through blogging
- forging partnerships with local higher education faculty
- pursuing independent research on good teaching, e.g., attending a conference on Reggio Emila
- developing new curriculum using the Next Generation Science Standards
- working with colleagues to move to Total Physical Response Storytelling to teach languages
- joining civic groups that enable teachers a voice at the policy-making table
- creating a code of ethics with colleagues
- taking a stand to refuse to administer high-stakes tests
- pursuing National Board Teacher Certification
- arranging a teaching schedule to ensure that students still take art, music, and physical education in the midst of faculty firings due to budget cuts
- getting release time through a foundation fellowship to research practice
- changing grade level or subject
- attending teacher-led protests

CHAPTER SIX

SCHOOL LEADERS: SOURCES OF DEMORALIZATION AND RE-MORALIZATION

"I've always been a rebel," Vanessa tells me. Lately, Vanessa has found *her voice through blogging and connecting with education activists from across the United States. She had entered a deep depression in her thirteenth year of teaching when she initially began bumping up against the standardization that was becoming the watchword in the affluent, suburban district where she works. Her school borders a major city in the Mid-Atlantic where she has a newfound solidarity with urban teach-ers who have been fighting the privatization of public schooling for over a decade. She recently attended an educational justice event in the city that forfeited this alliance.*

Now in her fourteenth year of middle school teaching, Vanessa is reenergized, but this is partly due to her hypervigilance against corporate involvement in public education. She can tell me where each district and building administrator has been trained, the sources of funding that support the various initiatives being rolled out in the schools, and the management techniques that consultants are deploying in their work with faculty.

Vanessa's assessment of her school leadership altered dramatically over the course of her tenure. In the first part of her career, she worked with a principal who demanded a lot from her faculty but ultimately trusted them. When Vanessa thought aloud about the kind of educational space she'd like to work in, her principal challenged her to write up a proposal. Diving into the opening presented by her school leader, Vanessa collaborated with another teacher and professors at a local university to develop a new team model that combined classes to focus on a specific area of inquiry. This program continues to draw students and has been replicated in other schools in the district.

With this principal, Vanessa believed that her voice was respected and heard, even when her ideas were not embraced. "We had big discussions as a grade level with an administrator once a week, or maybe once a month. We'd sit in a circle with an administrator and sometimes teachers get passionate. I wouldn't always agree, or I would say something, and people wouldn't always agree." Nonetheless, she believed that they usually found common ground by asking, "Is it good for kids? Let's do it if it's good for kids."

For the last several years, Vanessa's voice has been "muzzled." Faculty rarely engage in conversations about their work and do not have a chance to ask, "Is it good for kids?" Instead, they sit through slide-based presentations where they are told what is good for kids, and there are no opportunities to ask questions or offer alternatives. Teachers who want to ask a question or make a comment are encouraged to do so through an online form.

Vanessa describes the highly paid, well-educated faculty in this affluent suburban school as having "low morale" because "everything's fake and phony and prepackaged and scripted." In particular, Vanessa points to "forced PLCs" that she believes expect all members of a so-called professional learning community to develop the same products. She explains that she hopes that her colleagues will find creative space within these mandated work groups. "I want everyone to collaborate, but don't fall in line so much, you know? Do good work for kids, but don't be a robot. Question things."

Vanessa attributes what is happening in her school and district to market-based trends in education reform that are widespread across the country but have been felt most acutely in cities.

> *I probably spent a year and a half in a pretty deep depression about the attack on public education. And I felt stupid and naïve that I didn't see the attack on cities—that I just live so close and was in my suburban white privilege bubble. I mourned for the cities, I mourned for the families, the children. I mourned for all of us who have great schools, who are going to lose them. The quality of education was going down. What [the district and school leaders] were asking us to do didn't make sense.*

Vanessa sought to redress her ignorance and plunged into researching corporate-style reform of public education with the same fervor that she used to write a program proposal.

Finding no space to ask questions or to raise concerns in her school or district, Vanessa started blogging. Her blog provides a place to distill her research findings and connect initiatives and leadership approaches at her school with national policy trends. For instance, she has shown how punitive disciplinary practices and regimented pedagogies reserved typically for low-income students served by charter schools are starting to be utilized in her district: "I'll be damned if I want someone teaching my children or anybody's children like that." Realizing that these practices are damaging for all students, Vanessa uses her online voice to highlight the intertwined fates of suburban and urban districts. Online and in person, she forges alliances with teachers, parents, professors, and activists across the urban border.

Vanessa longs for the opportunities she once had with administrators who "welcomed discourse." She recalls, "I had an administrator who was interested in staff input. It was wonderful. You could really disagree on things. You could go into his office and he'd welcome you. He'd sit down with a pad of paper and he would take notes. He would think about what you were saying, and he would take action on things that he processed with you. If he didn't agree, he would say it." Now, she feels "underappreciated" and "invisible." "That's why people leave, you know? When they feel like nothing I do is heard or considered and it's demoralizing."

Vanessa views the attrition of veteran teachers as an intended effect of management styles that value compliance over critical thinking. It is a shame, she believes, because her district is uniquely rich in "intellectual resources." She and her colleagues resisted the imposition of simplistic explanations and the inability to engage with ideas. "They're saying things like 'Certainly, nobody can argue with that.' But, oh, I can argue that!" Vanessa believes that the district and school leadership are alienating experienced teachers when they present initiatives from a perspective of moral and practical certainty.

Vanessa's understanding of her moral center entails that she must always question her purposes and practices. Comparing her current teaching self to when she first entered the profession, she explains, "Now I have maturity, perspective, experience . . . I'm more aware of my professional ethics . . . I'll go down teaching right. Some teachers say, 'I'm just going to close my door and do the right thing,' which is important to do. But I feel like it wasn't enough for me. I'm a teacher and I want to educate my community." Refusing to take on the role of recluse, she uses her blog to fulfill her professional commitment to use her voice to reach beyond her classroom and school. Her blogs pose an insistent question: "Is this good for kids?"

Vanessa, a self-proclaimed rebel, presents school leaders with a pressing question. How do you harness the energy that this dedicated teacher brings to the school? Unabashedly outspoken, opinionated, and organized, Vanessa is also uncommonly passionate, dedicated, and willing to put in additional work for the good of the school and its students.

What happens when a teacher like Vanessa feels "muzzled" by her school and district leaders? Inexperienced school leaders initially may view Vanessa as a threat. They might interpret Vanessa's questioning and challenging as a sign that she is bound to undermine the priorities that they have envisioned for the school.

More seasoned school leaders might recognize Vanessa's assets and harness her energy. When Vanessa expressed displeasure with her classroom space, her first principal listened to her criticisms and invited Vanessa to write a proposal. The result was a collaboration with a local university to develop a program that has been replicated throughout the district. When recalling the productive relationship with this principal, Vanessa repeatedly remarked that she and the principal did not always agree but that they were able to communicate respectfully.

In contrast, Vanessa approached her current principal with a proposal to form a PLC with teachers in a similar program at another district school. Feeling as if she was spinning her wheels in her dysfunctional department's "fake" PLC with no clear purpose, she sought to find a productive resolution. Her inquiry was rejected without further discussion.

The current district and school leaders have not earned Vanessa's trust. They have not initiated, invited, or participated in conversations that addressed the question "Is this good for kids?" Vanessa perceives them as interlopers or pawns in projects originating outside her district and school. Most of the schoolwide initiatives and mandates are communicated through paid consultants. Vanessa finds few opportunities for teachers to ask questions or to provide feedback that might stimulate dialogue about the purposes or methods of the initiatives teachers are expected to implement. Instead, she and all other teachers who have questions are invited to make comments on an online form.

ACKNOWLEDGMENT OF TEACHERS' MORAL MOTIVATIONS

Experienced teachers like Vanessa are often suspicious of new school leaders, especially those who are younger than they. However, discrepancies in age and experience do not need to result in combative standoffs or unproductive stalemates. School leaders who engage teachers in conversations rooted in the question "Is this good for kids?" create opportunities for teachers to relate the expertise of their craft and their moral commitments to their work. Conflicts arise when school leaders presuppose that teachers lack expertise, moral motivations, and the desire to do good work. Vanessa begrudged her principal's out-of-hand rejection of her customized PLC request. She wanted to be productive, not waste time.

As discussed earlier, sociologist of teaching Daniel Lortie has shown that teachers articulate "normative," or moral, commitments about the well-being of their "clients" (students, families, communities) as well as the well-being of their profession. If school leaders ignore the moral dimension of teachers' concerns, they risk cutting off valuable communication that may yield common ground. What if school leaders recognized the significance of teachers' moral concerns, even while acknowledging moral disagreement might still prevail?

Vanessa explained that she has more fully developed her professional ethics over the course of her career. Throughout my time talking to Vanessa, I did not interpret this statement as an indication that her beliefs had become more rigid and fixed. Instead, I understood her as saying that she was more likely to look at her own teaching and the initiatives she was asked to enact through the question "Is this good for kids?" Vanessa has developed sophisticated criteria for what an affirmative answer is to that question. However, her development of a moral center should not be read as rigidity. She is still willing to ask "Is this good for kids?" and would like to engage in dialogue with her colleagues and leaders about the principles that motivate their policies and practices.

Facing a nationwide teacher shortage, school leaders must prioritize retaining and working effectively with experienced teachers. Positive school climate, for staff and students, depends on a satisfied and cooperative cadre of experienced teachers. When school leaders perceive teachers like Vanessa solely as obstacles to be overcome or liabilities that require damage control, they miss opportunities to enhance the school climate for all.

School leaders need training to improve working conditions at their schools and to improve teacher retention.[1] From a short-sighted management perspective, some school and district leaders might prefer novice teachers whose lower salaries provide relief to tight budgets and whose inexperience could translate into less resistance and influence. Yet, research shows that school climate and student performance improve when there is less teacher turnover.[2]

Overall, there is a dearth of research on experienced teachers and their beliefs about teaching; this allows images of veteran teachers as resistant to change and set in their outmoded ways to proliferate.[3] Partly, this gap can be attributed to a focus on the first five years of induction to the profession, when attrition is greatest. Another reason arises from research design. University-based researchers have easier access to early-career teachers who were once students. Even when experienced teachers are included in studies, the inquiry might not focus on beliefs about their work. Due to this gap in the research, in addition to the ageism that permeates US culture, stereotypical representations of veteran educators as unwilling or unable to innovate prevail.

School leaders commit a serious error when they interpret all teacher resistance as teachers' unwillingness to change or that their proposals seek to meet their self-serving needs. While these sources of resistance can be present in teaching (just as they may arise in any organization), they are not the only sources of teachers' dissatisfaction about their work.

MORAL BLACKMAIL AND MORAL MADNESS

Vanessa's dissatisfaction with teaching comes, in part, from an inability to engage in dialogue about her moral concerns with her extremely well-educated and accomplished colleagues and their school leaders. She is stupefied by policies that appear to come out of nowhere and are justified simplistically as *the* way to serve all students. The result is that she and her colleagues have faced the equivalent of moral blackmail. When school leaders (or, in Vanessa's case, the consultants) present new mandates as the only answer to meeting the needs of students, they may deploy the language of meeting students' needs, or inclusion, or rigor to shame teachers into compliance.

Multiple teachers described experiences of moral blackmail when they questioned mandates and raised concerns about the implications of their implementation. The titles of the initiatives themselves can be phrased in ways that place teachers in a moral bind. For instance, the title of scripted curricula like *Success for All* may place critics on the defensive. Teachers who question the efficacy and value of this corporate product may find themselves addressing accusations that they do not want success for all.

Experienced teachers described having the latest educational buzzwords weaponized. A veteran teacher who participated in a re-moralization retreat recounted how her principal used this strategy to shut down dialogue about the ways that standards-based grading was being implemented. She reminded teachers that they must have a "growth mindset." When school leaders turn important conceptual frameworks, like Carol Dweck's theory of mindset, into a weapon for compliance, they lose opportunities to utilize concepts that could help educators better discuss, plan, interpret, and assess their work. A growth mindset does not entail unquestioning compliance, and its usefulness and significance to teachers' work become diminished, or even meaningless, when the term is deployed in this way.

The moral landscape of education has been winnowed by the important, but limited, language of achievement that eviscerates full moral discourse about teaching. In a morally constrained pedagogical policy environment, teachers' criticisms regarding pedagogical policy are cast in binary terms, either for or against the proposed initiative. Teacher researchers Betty Achinstein and Rodney Ogawa explain that this current form of "moralistic control compounds the stifling effect that technical control can have on teacher reflection, discussion, and debate of instructional practice."[4]

Elsewhere, I have described the environment in which teachers currently work as "morally constrained."[5] It is a policy environment in which only one version of what counts as moral is valued or entertained. Within this logic, criticism by teachers is cast as immoral or self-serving. For instance, New York State Commissioner of Education MaryEllen Elia has characterized any teacher who criticized state tests as "unethical."[6] Teachers' moral concerns may be described by school leaders as either unsupportive of the stated equity goals of pedagogical policies or as personal resistance to change and growth. Both imputed stances leave teachers with little moral ground from which to articulate and defend their concerns about the profession. This is a particular problem when teachers lose moral credibility whenever they engage in criticism of pedagogical policy.

Diane's experience in the preceding chapter provides a vivid example of the ways that the discourse of educational policy can become weaponized when it is placed on an unimpeachable moral high ground. Diane was publicly censured by her principal for speaking out against high-stakes testing. He and the district leadership characterized her actions as "unprofessional." However, Diane understood her behavior as coming from a place of profound professional responsibility. By disregarding her voicing her moral center as "unprofessional," he negated her ability to be viewed as someone who possesses professional ethics.

The erasure of Diane's moral agency and the description of her actions as "unprofessional" may provoke moral madness. Moral madness, I have argued elsewhere, is a symptom of moral violence.[7] The violence occurs when an individual is not recognized as a moral agent or when an individual makes a moral claim that is refused to be recognized as moral. This is what happened to Diane when she presented her case to parents about opting out of high-stakes tests. Moral recognition does not need to entail agreement. Yet, the leaders in Diane's school and district instead rendered her moral concerns as not morally motivated.

Despite there being little dispute that teaching is a moral profession and that teachers are expected to conduct themselves as moral exemplars, teachers may find that they struggle to achieve recognition as moral agents. In fact, Domain 4 of the Danielson assessment model used by many states rewards teachers who act as advocates for their students and the profession. This behavior is grouped with other professional and ethical indicators.

The moral claims of teachers, I argue, are often not examined alongside the moral claims of leaders or policy makers, but are rendered irrelevant, and even immoral, by those with more institutional power. Because current policy sets itself up as moral in that it seeks to remedy unequal educational outcomes, and this is a worthy goal of legislation, it renders all other criticism as immoral or only personal and selfish.

RE-MORALIZATION BY PRINCIPAL

School leaders have much to gain if they acknowledge teachers' moral commitments and engage teachers in discussions about their moral concerns. When this happens, regardless of the ultimate policy decisions, school leaders and teachers can be engaged together in the practice of professional ethics. In chapter 3, DeeDee was left demoralized. She had ceded her professional responsibility to her grade-level colleagues and submerged her expertise in math education to be "part of a team." Here is where we left DeeDee, but it is not how her career is going to end. A school leader acknowledged the moral source of DeeDee's curricular concerns and altered her career trajectory.

The effects of teaching the textbook with fidelity demoralized DeeDee. Gone were the days when her students named math as their favorite subject. She felt dead to her teaching, and she worried that by teaching with the textbook, she lost the ability to help students fall in love with math and explore its concepts more deeply. "I left my soul out of the picture for a few years. That's an easy way to say it. My passion was gone. My teaching soul was gone. It was almost like that drugged feeling where you just do what they tell you to do. And you don't have any fight left in you."

She planned on just following the rules and distancing herself from the work she was doing. It hurt less that way. Retirement wasn't too far off.

After thirty-five years of developing expertise in math pedagogy, DeeDee had become resigned to bringing a much-reduced version of herself to the classroom for the final years of her career. Surreptitiously, she would use an inquiry-based math approach during unstructured time in her class, usually only once or twice per week. A visitor researching math pedagogy observed DeeDee's approach to teaching math and asked her why she didn't use it all the time. The conversation with the visitor led DeeDee to wonder, "I'm supposed to be part of a team, but I left that afternoon going, Can you be part of a team in a different way? Can you have yourself back? Can you have your soul back?" The visitor gave DeeDee the inspiration to approach Amy, her new principal, and ask if she could stop using the textbook. "And [Amy's] response was, 'Do you want help setting the bonfire?' And I just said," sighed DeeDee, "I think I even said it out loud. 'I love you.'"

Amy, a school leader whose age comes closer to DeeDee's years of teaching experience, was able to listen to DeeDee and hear that she did not want to use the textbook due to moral concerns, not a self-serving resistance to change. In another school or district, Amy may not have had the latitude to endorse DeeDee's abandoning the textbook. In a more restrictive situation, the conversation, based in acknowledgment of teacher expertise and a shared concern for professional ethics, likely could have yielded creative alternatives. At the very least, a conversation that acknowledges the moral motivations of some teacher resistance can support the mutual recognition of shared values and commitments, such as meeting the needs of students and the responsibilities of professional educators.

To reiterate, DeeDee experienced demoralization, not burnout. DeeDee was still excited about teaching math, and she possessed the skills and ability to engage young children in mathematical concepts. Her dilemma was not how to teach math well, but that she felt she could not teach math well given the pedagogical mandates that had been established. DeeDee felt that she had "lost her soul" when she could not give her students the best learning experiences that she was able to provide. Now, after thirty-five years of teaching, she had her soul back.

DeeDee is not the only teacher whose work was re-moralized as a result of her school leader. Wanting to pursue a teacher leadership role, Hilary (chapter 3) was supported in applying for a fellowship that allowed her to have a hybrid role in her school. This opportunity launched her into research about teacher-led schools. With the support of her school and district leaders and an educational foundation, Hilary plans to launch a teacher-led model in her district.

Growing stale after twenty years of teaching, Yesi (chapter 5) was prepared to transfer to another school because she needed to try something new. When the science teaching position opened in the early grades, Yesi's principal offered her the job. While Yesi has been learning, sometimes with tears as feedback, about how to gear her lessons appropriately to the school's earliest grades, the move has re-energized and re-moralized her. She is quickly becoming a leader in aligning the district's curriculum to the Next Generation Science Standards.

School leaders have the potential to re-moralize teachers' work, but this process requires that teachers are able to have their moral concerns heard. At the very least, it behooves district leaders to investigate whether teachers' moral concerns contribute to attrition in their schools. My past research revealed that when experienced teachers left teaching due to moral concerns about their work, not a single school leader asked, "What could we do to address your concerns?" or "What would it take for you to stay?" Furthermore, not a single teacher was given an exit interview.

SOURCES OF DEMORALIZATION

Just as school leaders can be the source of teacher re-moralization, they also can be the source of demoralization. Not asking teachers with years of service to a school what could be done to retain them is a prime example of professional disregard that can lead to demoralization, even for teachers who stay. In a number of incidents, school or district leaders behaved in ways that exceeded the bounds of professional behavior or revealed extremely poor judgment. Quinn's principal (chapter 2) retaliated against him over the school loudspeaker while classes were in session. Yesi's first principal humiliated her in front of students (chapter 5). Monica's principal leveled accusations of abusing a student just before she needed to teach her students (chapter 3). Edwin's principal failed to acknowledge his application for a leadership position and asked him to alter students' grades (chapter 4). Vanessa's school and district leadership deflected conversations to an online portal (this chapter).

School leaders communicate their beliefs about the dignity of the profession directly and indirectly. While few school leaders would disparage teaching outright, they do denigrate the profession when experienced teachers in their school do not know what they will be teaching with fewer than three weeks before the beginning of the school year. This was the case for Marnie and Edwin (both in chapter 4). Even though personnel instability or enrollment insecurity may make predicting teaching assignments challenging on occasion, this situation, which many teachers experience as a norm, communicates that teachers do not prepare in advance and that any teacher is interchangeable with any other. Teachers described their sense of professional indignity when colleagues with more seniority can bump another teacher from their placement, as was the case in districts such as Marnie's, Diane's (chapter 5), Carla's (chapter 3), and Patty's (discussed in this chapter).

Nearly all teachers referenced the Danielson model for teacher assessment. Many found the domains to be "copyrighted common sense" and were comfortable with the parameters on which they would be evaluated. However, Gina (chapter 4) reported that preparing a pre-observation document alone required over twelve hours of work. As budget and curricular pressures winnow opportunities for teacher planning, collaboration, and independent work during the school day, school leaders need to be vigilant about unnecessarily contributing to the intensification of teachers' work. Teachers were demoralized by having to spend time on tasks that did not appear to improve their practice or enable them to better serve students.

Nearly all the teachers with whom I spoke discussed the labor that they put into developing achievement goals for their students known as student learning objectives (SLOs). As I traveled to several different states, I was struck by the uniformity of the supposedly state-level expectations. Furthermore, the teachers described nearly identical processes of directives from school and district leaders, teacher confusion, and intense teacher investment in fulfilling the expectation. The process concluded with school and district leaders letting teachers know that the intense period of labor was unnecessary and that they would provide the language and formula for the SLOs.

Most teachers received no training on developing SLOs. However, they knew that these metrics were incredibly important because they were the measures that would, in part, determine evaluation rankings as well as merit pay, in some states. The teachers wanted to do their jobs well but were at a loss as to what made a good SLO. For many, the process proved even more frustrating because after they spent dozens of hours puzzling over and crafting SLOs (instead of meeting with students, planning curriculum, or responding to student work), districts then informed teachers that the SLOs were actually formulaic and required a template statement that negated the value of all their prior work.

Recall Gina's experience:

Gina scoured over student records trying to anticipate the projected learning outcomes she could expect for students whom she had yet to meet. "I had to come home and use these tests where all of [the students] failed and figure out how to predict how many would pass in June. My husband said, 'You're crying again.' I care about teaching, and I felt like this was part of teaching. And I was literally crying every night for a month, a full month. As this district and the school and the state figured out what these things were meaning, they kept changing it. They kept saying, 'Oh, no, it actually means this . . .' And then it turned out to be a total BS phrase that we were all supposed to copy from each other that basically said 60 percent of my kids will get a 65 or above . . ."

Teachers expressed significant concerns about initiatives, especially technological ones that created additional, unnecessary labor. They were livid about software applications that sent precious resources out of the school or district but were cumbersome, rolled out too soon, and had insufficient support from the developer. Teachers like Patty, who has taught for sixteen years, reported spending dozens of hours after school entering student data into a program that could have been patched in by the central office or the publisher.

She also took it on herself to train her building in the report card software. A self-proclaimed rule follower, she does the work even when she is not sure about the purpose. Some initiatives made her a better teacher, but she questioned the value of one of the several assessments she administers each month: "I'm sitting there and entering that data into a program, I don't even know who looks at it. I know I have to do it and I do it, and I do it on time. And if I'm supposed to give a test every two weeks, I give a test every two weeks. I did it today. It's in my plan book."

Patty has been working in urban elementary schools in a Midwestern district for thirteen of her sixteen years of teaching. This is her second career, and she takes mandates in stride. Even though she works three jobs to maintain a lifestyle focused on travel during her breaks from school, she assiduously completes new requirements that come her way. This year, however, the level of documentation that the district requires has overwhelmed her.

"The paperwork is a low point for me," Patty explains. She quickly enumerates a staggering array of tasks. "I am being asked to cocreate and enter intervention [response to intervention (RTI)] plans for my lower students in math and reading. I test those students biweekly [in math and reading] and the data is entered on the computer. Report cards, grade book, parent contact logs." Fluidly, she moves into the new assessments that her grade-level team is writing to align with Common Core reading standards, then two new curricula that the district just adopted. The new curricula come with new computer-based assessments that she must administer at regular intervals.

Patty's very excited about the depth that she can go into subjects on account of Common Core. She appreciates the kind of feedback that she receives from the computer-based assessments. "They're making me a better teacher; it's helped me identify [student needs] better. You have to enter all that data in, so it's a lot of work, but it's very valuable." She is not sure that all of the scanning she needs to complete in order to submit artifacts for her teacher evaluations is making her a better teacher, however. Patty has yet to see the value in entering all the data for RTI plans and biweekly assessments into the computer, but she believes the targeted instruction helps the students, so she is happy to do it.

"Ooh, I forgot!" Patty interjects. She now recalls that the district requires her to develop SLOs and articulate a professional practice goal (PPG). Hers is to "have more hands-on engaging math lessons." She's excited about articulating and pursuing this development in her teaching, but she is not motivated by the ways that SLOs will be tied to her compensation. "If I've done my best, and I don't meet my SLO, that's just fine by me."

"I don't know where a lot of these things [initiatives like SLOs] come from, to be honest with you. I mean, I was in business for a long time. [I recognize that] the other side of the coin is teachers aren't held very accountable for too much, you know. So how do you change that? This accountability was awful. How do you make teachers accountable, and what's the best way? I don't know if that's something that can be solved. I don't think it can be solved in a year."

The teachers I interviewed took their jobs seriously. Even if they did not understand the purpose of a task (in the case of SLOs) or were provided with insufficient resources with which to perform the task well, they described the lengths they went to do good work. Many teachers mentioned the fatigue that accompanies a rotating slate of initiatives and technology innovations. School and district leaders could find ways to protect their staff's time. A number of teachers' experiences suggested that the haste in introducing new computer applications expected teachers to do work that would have been better handled by the software developer's employees or the district's operations staff.

None of my interview questions focused on leadership, but almost all the teachers mentioned the ways in which school and district leaders were significant sources of demoralization and re-moralization in their careers. These responses suggest that much more research is needed to understand the ways that school and district leaders contribute to the moral sources of teacher satisfaction and dissatisfaction. This feedback also indicates that school and district leaders need to better acquaint themselves with the moral motivations that many teachers bring to their work. As is said in special education circles, understanding teachers' moral commitments to their students and to the dignity of their profession may be the "least dangerous assumption."

The teachers I interviewed often expressed empathy toward their school leaders. They recognize that school leaders face an onslaught of mandates and intense pressures from various constituencies, often without the same employment protections teachers may enjoy. Every teacher I interviewed preferred productive and collaborative relationships with their school leaders. They were in agreement that effective school leaders enacted a clear vision, valued teachers and their experience, and investigated teacher dissent or resistance. The best school leaders acted as gatekeepers of policies and mandates, assessed them in relation to the school's vision, and sheltered teachers and students from an onslaught of rotating initiatives.

Here, then, are some recommendations for school leaders who care about improving teacher satisfaction and retention:

- Listen for, recognize, and respond to teachers' moral concerns.
- Facilitate discussions about what good teaching looks like. Learn what faculty members believe enables them to and prevents them from engaging in good teaching. Ask teachers what they need to engage in good teaching.
- Become curious about teachers' resistance. Teachers value administrators who provide opportunities for them to use their voices and expertise, even when they do not ultimately agree.
- School board members can institute a listen-to-teachers tour throughout the state/district.
- Separate federal, state, and district initiatives into three categories: nonnegotiable, desirable, and better-off-ignored. Protect teachers from unnecessary new initiatives. Sustain focus on the initiatives that advance the goals and mission of the school. Communicate the relationship between the mission and goals to the expectations you have for faculty.
- Practice teacher-led principles, even in traditionally governed schools.
- Create hybrid roles for teachers to exercise leadership while remaining in the classroom. Only three of the twenty-two teachers interviewed were interested in moving into non-teaching leadership roles. Hybrid and leadership roles work best if they are coupled with a limited teaching load.
- Institute exit interviews and collect data on why teachers leave a school or district voluntarily. A teacher working in a hybrid role may collect the best data.
- Enable teachers to exercise choice regarding topic and composition in their professional learning communities. Consider expanding professional learning communities beyond the school building.

- Differentiate professional development to meet needs across the career span.
- Share responsibility for difficult decisions with teachers (e.g., passing or suspending students). Avoid passing the buck.
- Establish an ombudsperson for the district.

CHAPTER SEVEN

TEACHER UNIONS: SOURCES OF DEMORALIZATION AND RE-MORALIZATION

*O*n my ride out to the south side of Chicago, I imagined the person I was about to meet. Frank would be fiery, combative, tough, and fiercely committed to the profession. I knew that he wrote a blog about teaching and race on a national online news outlet. Frank's writing is insistent, demanding, and unflinchingly honest. I expected the same energy from his in-person presence.

While Frank delivered in being fiercely committed to his profession, I learned quickly during our conversation that he is even more devoted to his students and his family. He is gentle, self-effacing, and demanding in his expectation that he enable students to make sense of their lives in his classroom. Justice, for Frank, isn't a remote ideal. It is a felt imperative that motivates his choices about where to live and work and how to embody the roles of husband, father, son, teacher, and community member.

Despite being untenured, Frank felt confident taking on his school's union delegate role early in his career because he trusted the principal. He noticed that she followed the rules and referred to the union handbook. Looking back, he admitted that he wasn't sure what he was getting into. Nonetheless, someone needed to take on the role. Frank's the guy who is not going to let a job be left undone.

He recalled feeling alienated by union meeting agendas and conversations that bore little resemblance to the questions and issues that urgently required attention in his school. However, when Chicago Teachers Union [CTU] President Karen Lewis took the helm and delivered a message of social justice unionism, Frank took notice of the change. "When I first started [with the union], before Karen Lewis was the current CTU president, I was like, 'What the hell are these meetings?' Then, she came in and I was like, 'Oh, you're talking about really making schools better. And, you're also caring about the rights of gay students, and you care what's going on in Honduras.'" Frank wanted to be involved in a union that brought the problems faced by teachers and students locally and globally under one umbrella.

The shift in the union's message altered Frank's level of engagement in the CTU. The union "started caring about everything and really caring about our kids. [The message was that we need to] care about ourselves, too, but it wasn't just money and benefits." As his involvement in the union deepened, Frank started learning more about the role of unions and union members in effecting social change. Identifying a historical narrative enabled Frank to see the significance of his participation in the union.

One way that Frank embodied his role as a union member was to make his teaching public and transparent. He explains, "Being the union delegate, I felt a moral responsibility to be like 'Here's what I'm doing in my classroom' publicly." With his first principal, this stance posed no threats of insubordination or significant risk to his employment. The second principal expected deference rather than reasoned rationales. The pedagogical choices Frank made in good professional conscience contradicted the principal's directives. His practice of making his teaching public now appeared defiant. "The last few years before I left were focused on testing. [The message from the school leaders was] we only care about testing. Test prep. Test prep. Test prep. I would send out e-mails to just the teaching staff saying, 'I'm not going to do test prep. I'm going to teach. I'm going to make sure that my kids are learning skills they need to learn, but they're not going to sit there and do test prep.'"

These communiques, when Frank's first principal was at the helm, would stimulate substantive conversations in faculty meetings. These meetings might result in teachers finding alternatives to test prep in order to build students' skills. Teachers were given opportunities to meet in departments and by grade level to determine where they could close skill and content gaps. However, the second principal provided no space or time for faculty collaboration or dialogue about policy. The unilateralism of the second principal drove Frank more deeply into his union involvement and eventually led him to seek another position. He also began entertaining the idea of becoming a principal. He had witnessed the enormous impact a leader can have on the quality of teaching and climate in a school.

Frank's increased involvement in the union coincided with the 2012 CTU strike. Leading up to the strike, Frank initiated conversations with his students and their families about the problems they perceived in their schools. While the union could legally strike only on the issues of salary and benefits, Frank and other delegates found that students' and families' concerns aligned with their own as educators. Union members, like Frank, found ways to counteract the "greedy teachers" narrative and articulate shared concerns across stakeholders prior to initiating the strike. The teachers held a practice picket line at the school in May, and it provided another opportunity to communicate with the public, including students, about the teachers' concerns. Frank ensured that his classes were able to articulate arguments for and against the strike.

Frank sees the union as providing a voice for students as well as teachers. Reflecting on the challenges facing Chicago Public Schools—mayoral control, the absence of an elected school board, and the six different leaders of CPS in eight years—Frank remarks, "I mean the kids are who are really getting screwed over." He recalls a recent school closing hearing where thousands of people packed a huge auditorium. "Little kids are talking about 'please don't close our schools because we have this great program.' I mean thousands of people are yelling at CPS, but CPS wouldn't let them talk, wouldn't answer questions."

In the face of what Frank views as an unresponsive organization are real people inhabiting schools and communities with immediate needs. He explains, "The per pupil funding is just morally wrong. In the school I used to work at, we had a nurse for half a day on Fridays. That was it. We had a library with no librarian. We had one social worker. One counselor in one of the most violent neighborhoods. Excuse my language, but just shit you wouldn't want done to your family or your friend's family. Now I think about it as a father, I'm like, are you kidding me? . . . As teachers, we have to speak up for our kids."

Understanding that the union also protected the profession, not just the employment of individual teachers, came more slowly. Frank had not realized that his first job in Chicago was at a turnaround school. At a social justice conference, Frank met the person whose position he occupied after all the faculty were dismissed when the school was restructured. Frank sat with the irony and the embarrassment of meeting this person at a union-sponsored social justice gathering. This experience was part of a constellation of events that opened Frank's eyes to the politics of school reform in Chicago. He began to develop a consciousness as a member of a profession and an understanding of the role a union might play in both protecting its members and articulating and upholding professional principles.

As significant as the union has been to Frank's sense of empowerment and moral center as a teacher, he is not currently as engaged in the CTU as he once was. After two years of working with a principal with whom he clashed in terms of school priorities and leadership approach, Frank transferred to another school in the south side of Chicago. He believes that his active union involvement impeded his job search, and he is currently more cautious about how he is making his voice heard. Frank continues to write for a national online news outlet but is circumspect about taking on another leadership role in the union.

Frank thinks his trouble transferring to another school derives from a widespread assumption that "you get viewed as a good union person or a good teacher. People don't view it as you can be both." He was granted interviews only after removing his union involvement from his resume. In pursuing National Board Teacher Certification (NBTC) this year, Frank aims to show that being a strong union person and a great teacher are not mutually exclusive. He hopes that NBTC might provide him with an added layer of pedagogical and moral authority when he needs to take a stand. He also believes that NBTC will provide him with a bit of a reality check. "It would prove to me, too, that if I applied for another school and I am not getting interviews [that] people are afraid of the outspoken teacher as opposed to not being qualified. Because that messed with me, and it still messes with me. It bothers me." It is difficult for Frank to digest the fact that a school leader would rather take a substandard teacher than a strong teacher who was engaged in union activity.

This first year at a new school, Frank is committed to keeping his head down. He will focus on teaching—no serving as union delegate, *no working as department chair, no coaching spoken word. Just work on being a great teacher. I wondered if that limited, classroom-based view of teaching was possible for a guy like Frank. I said it aloud, "I'm curious how long you'll contain your voice."*

"You know," replied Frank, "I do, too."

Frank's engagement with the union remained superficial until he heard CTU President Karen Lewis's message that the union and its members are advocates for students, public schools, and their communities. He could not commit to deeper involvement when the union seemed to care solely about the well-being of individual teachers. When concerns about social justice and the teaching profession coalesced under the auspices of the union leadership's focused message, Frank found a way to live and communicate his professional commitments on a grander scale.

As a teacher motivated by issues of justice and community, the union's initial focus on individual teachers' rights and benefits did not resonate as relevant or reasonable, especially when Frank compared those to the needs his students faced in his classroom. The union leadership also effectively identified the talents in its membership. Frank would not be the person to rally a crowd with a megaphone, but given a platform for writing, his voice would travel.

While Frank did not need a union to help him articulate his professional values, his involvement with the CTU enabled him to amplify his voice. As building delegate, he shared his teaching principles and practices with his faculty through e-mail messages, regular meetings (some were facilitated by his first principal), and an open-door policy. After he wrote hundreds of letters to newspaper editors, a union organizer gave him a much wider platform by connecting him to a national online news outlet where he now has an audience of millions.

Becoming involved in the union provided Frank with an education that he passed on to students. The union offered Frank a framework to make sense of Chicago's school governance and education policy, especially in terms of how it affected students, teachers, and their communities.

He learned about the historical contributions that unions and their members had made in advancing social change and advocating for justice. Frank developed skills about organizing communities that he used to shape and share the message of the CTU strike.

Social justice unionism takes the well-being of all in a community as its concern. The strategies for organizing are available to all, not only those with a union membership. When students undertook what Frank calls "the most poorly planned [protest] I've ever seen" to lodge a complaint about the school's heating system, he designed a series of lessons to teach them how to protest more effectively.

CAUTIOUS ASSOCIATIONS

Just as with school leaders, teachers recounted that their union could be a source of demoralization and an opportunity for re-moralization. Teachers, like Frank, felt disconnected and disheartened with their union when they perceived it as promoting organizational interests over advocacy for teachers and students. However, many also commented that opportunities available in the union enabled them to build professional allies, a sense of purpose, and enriched connections with their communities.

Sometimes, serving as a union building representative or delegate created untenable conditions and employability challenges. Participation in union governance posed a risk for Frank and others, like Quinn, whose experience was described in chapter 2. The effects of punitive education reform such as turnaround schools, usually limited to urban districts with high-need student populations, decimates experienced faculties and, with it, seasoned union leadership.

When building representative or delegate roles are taken up by untenured faculty who are more vulnerable in terms of employment status and are still establishing themselves professionally, they may face substantial hiring hurdles in the future. When this happens, the union may meet short-term needs at the expense of well-meaning but inexperienced teachers. Even mid-career teachers like Frank may find that strong union ties hamper their future employment prospects.

While there may be no way to eliminate assumptions employers may make about union-affiliated employees, teacher unions could anticipate and attempt to attenuate challenges faced by their members. Unions might consider other mechanisms to ensure union representation in buildings where no suitable tenured member is able to serve. One possibility could be a union mentorship program that offers classroom-based support to new teachers while providing building representation. Retired members might be particularly well suited for positions like these as a form of professional service. In cities where tense relationships between the union, school leaders, and elected officials are the norm, union leadership and experienced peers could coach members about ways to account for the skills developed and service rendered through union activity without unnecessarily jeopardizing their employment prospects.

Jason checked his phone intermittently throughout our conversation. He was waiting to hear if he was elected to a leadership position at his school. Already he has made himself an invaluable asset to the school, which helps when he's in the midst of thorny relations with his school leadership. Jason has coached multiple sports teams; works on a school-level team to ensure students are being appropriately challenged by their course selections; and serves on another school-level team that supports students facing social-emotional, drug, and/or alcohol challenges. He has mentored student teachers. Jason is the union representative for his building and is a local teacher leader for his national union.

Jason teaches in an urban district because he loves it. He supplements his salary with summer landscaping work in order to support his family. He grew up in what he describes as an "anti-union house, attending religious schools which aren't really keen on unions." Yet, he decided to "get engaged with the union . . . If it's not going to change from outside, maybe we can upend it from within." He and some colleagues started a rank-and-file campaign against the local union leadership. Losing by a narrow margin, Jason has noticed that the leaders have become more receptive to members who share his concerns. Getting involved with the union is all about trying to repair it from the inside. Jason said, "I don't know for sure if the union's primary purpose right now is protecting me or protecting its own power." Although he sees his union as flawed, Jason wants to use it to leverage power.

Ask a question about educational policy, governance, or philanthropic involvement in Jason's urban district, and he'll help you connect the dots. He distinguishes himself from his colleagues who "just teach" and by high-lighting his dedication to uncovering the network of influence and impact in the city's schools. The city's student population has declined dramatically due to a loss of industry over the past fifty years, but it benefits from a vibrant cultural scene and many institutions of higher education.

The city's schools have been a focal point for studies and initiatives conducted by so-called research arms of philanthropic organizations and nearby universities. Over $80 million was pumped into the district to reform teacher evaluation. Jason is the first to admit that prior to the initiative, he had witnessed no systematic supports to assess and improve teacher performance. "We needed a change," he explained. Some of the elements of the new evaluation program had the potential to lead to improvements in teaching. However, he distinguished what was being measured and rewarded in the evaluation process from an articulation of good teaching. Jason unpacks the validity of the district's current measures for teacher effectiveness and merit pay. He unabashedly discusses his role in subverting their validity.

In his role as union rep, Jason felt a responsibility to help coworkers understand the stakes and how to game what he understood to be a flawed evaluation process. The goal of the evaluation system, he learned, was to fire 15 percent of the district's teachers. "I told everybody in my building, 'Rank yourself distinguished on every category and tell them to prove that you're not.' That's terrible for teacher growth. Teacher growth relies on honesty and systematic reflection. But your evaluation system tells you if you can pay your mortgage." The premise of firing 15 percent of teachers in an urban district struck Jason as remarkably unsound, especially in a low-status and poorly paid profession. He hypothesized that the effects of this punitive evaluation model would be to drive the better teachers into the higher-salary suburbs and leave the city district understaffed by qualified teachers.

As part of the evaluation process, Jason's union successfully negotiated for building-level climate surveys about the teaching and learning environment. Principals were expected to utilize the results in their annual planning reports. Through this feedback mechanism, the teachers were able to eliminate the district's mandated scripted curriculum. Jason argued that the curriculum "wasn't good for kids," but the worst aspect was that the "terrible" materials were required only for the "mainstream and remedial students."[1] He focused on the injustice. "These are the kids that needed more engagement. One of the reasons they didn't mess with the gifted curriculum was because the parents would have slaughtered [the district leaders] before it even came out. Somebody would have e-mailed the curriculum to a parent; they would have a little house party and said, 'This is the curriculum.' They would have slammed down their wine glasses and marched down to the Board of Ed, saying 'We're not sending our kids to your schools.' They buy crap for the needy kids."

Jason began to connect the dots between the Gates Foundation money that was funding the district's teacher evaluation redesign and Teach For America. The plan to fire 15 percent of the teaching force would manufacture a teacher shortage. Several universities in the district had teacher education programs whose graduates clamored for positions in the city. Jason had just returned from a Gates-funded conference that felt like a lavish vacation. "We get a chance to stay in a hotel that I would never stay in. There was an infinity pool! That's not what happens in normal life for me." While he was there, he was really excited to talk about college readiness. He recalled, "This is really high interest for me, but then they start talking about this 'effective teacher' stuff and it just smells weird."

Although Jason had used Twitter in the past, he mostly used it for entertainment, following sports-related news. He started live-tweeting the conference and followed the presenters. He began to realize that everyone presenting was connected to Teach For America. "I start a list. I'm at this conference and in my hotel room at night and look up everyone in [my district's] central office. I'm looking them up: Teach For America, Broad Institute. It's sort of like weird bunnies replicating at district head-quarters. All of the talking points are about closing schools, effective teaching, and buzzwords like "rigor." Everything's sort of clicking. The plane lands on a Friday. On Saturday, buried in the paper, is that [our city] has a hiring crisis and we're going to hire Teach For America."

Along with a union organizer and some colleagues, Jason organized a press conference to expose the contradiction in the resources to improve *teacher effectiveness and giving Teach For America a contract in the city. "We can't talk about teacher effectiveness and talk about investing in [the city's] teachers—which was what the Gates grant was supposed to do. We can't talk about that and hire temps. Doesn't make sense." Their efforts included coordinated protests at city hall and at the board of education meetings. Teach For America was not awarded a contract with the city. Teachers in the district became engaged and activated when they learned that they had to protect their profession, not just their own jobs.*

It might appear that Jason lacks a moral center when he takes the ethically dubious tack of recommending that his fellow teachers game the teacher evaluation system. However, Jason draws a clear distinction between an evaluative process that affects contracts and remuneration and one that yields constructive feedback for improving teaching practice. His distinction echoes Gina's concern, described in chapter 4, about the evaluative rankings. "All of us should be developing," she remarked. Unfortunately, that designation, while appropriate for the growth mindset that teachers are encouraged to foster in their students and the ideal for professional learning, has negative effects for all teachers when applied to a system intended to determine salary increases and contract renewals.

Contrast Jason's disposition with DeeDee's, described in chapter 3. Jason echoes DeeDee's unease with "managed curriculum," but with a dramatically different approach. Jason, unlike rule-following DeeDee, is a rebel. He pulled no punches when criticizing the mandated scripted literature program. His supervisor attempted to placate him by suggesting that he treat the managed curriculum "like a recipe." Jason then extended the metaphor. He said, "What you gave us was a recipe for vomit and so we won't make that again. That's what you do with a recipe that tastes like this curriculum, you just don't make it anymore." Jason explained that the "recipe" of the scripted curriculum did not engage his students in literature, and it damaged the learning environment he worked hard to establish.

Jason was also able to take a strong stance in relation to his school leader by strategically filling various service positions that were necessary for the school to function. He uses his role in the union to generate support for and protect the things he cares about most in teaching: high-quality pedagogy and justice for all students, especially the most vulnerable who have little social and political capital. He prizes the teaching profession and is willing to defend it against those who cheapen it through what he sees as misguided experimentation or nefarious doublespeak. Jason's commitment to teaching reaches well beyond the classroom into all kinds of cocurricular supports for students.

A good deal of Jason's political education has come from the action research that has been sponsored by his union. He recognizes that sometimes his union makes concessions in order to get a seat at the bargaining table. This practice enabled the union to require building-level teaching and learning environment surveys as part of the Gates-funded teacher evaluation overhaul. These surveys provided an outlet for teachers to roundly criticize the district's scripted curriculum. Because these surveys were included in building administrators' annual evaluations, they became a mechanism by which teachers could improve teaching and learning.

As a teacher leader with his local union chapter, Jason was able to meet other engaged educators in his district and participate in action research. Through this initiative, his union linked professional community, teacher voice, teacher leadership, and student-centered activity. This combination is an especially powerful antidote to demoralization and offers a strategy for re-moralization that unions are well positioned to support.

CHANGE FROM WITHIN

Jason recognized that he raised a perennial question that could be posed to any labor union: Is the union meeting the needs of its members or primarily interested in preserving its power as an organization? Jason was willing to tolerate some of his qualms with the union to ensure that its priorities, at least at the most local level, aligned with his values about teaching.

For some teachers, union collaboration with philanthrocapitalists, like Gates, reeks of capitulation rather than cooperation. Teachers like Vanessa (chapter 6) felt let down or betrayed by their union. By accepting Gates Foundation funds, she feels as though the very people who are supposed to protect the core values of the profession have sold out. "Our state union and our national union took Gates money. We have no great unions. And there's just so much [anti-union] propaganda out there, but they're very, very weak."

The unions may lose credibility from their members who are becoming more politically attuned about the role of private capital in public education. Online movements such as the Badass Teachers Association (BATs), United Opt Out (UOO), and the Network for Public Education (NPE), which includes high-profile public scholars and bloggers such as Diane Ravitch and Anthony Cody, are raising consciousness among teachers. While not anti-union, these independent associations of teachers and their allies are willing to point out union collaborations that may raise some concerns from the perspective of transparency, democracy, and teacher professionalism.

Teachers who have been "following the money" that influences reform have trouble viewing philanthropy as neutral or beneficial when the same organization seems to undermine the teaching profession. Vanessa considered it hypocritical that her union would accept funding from a source that also promotes antiunion and antiteacher initiatives. Helen (chapter 4) believes that the unions have negotiated to the point that they have compromised the integrity of the work teachers do.

> I think our unions have been bought out to a certain degree; they've been complicit in the standardization. Nobody wanted to say we don't believe in standards. Of course not. So they went along, they tried to compromise, you know sort of shape this whole, runaway train . . . I think in that process, a lot of compromises, serious ethical compromises, were made, and then it almost became too late. I mean like we're now in a position where we're overtesting kids so extensively across the country and teachers now, the majority of teachers that I see, don't really feel like they have the right to complain. They're just holding on. They need their jobs.

Here, Helen points out that the union has failed on both normative commitments Daniel Lortie explains are of importance to teachers: obligations to do the best by their students and to uphold the dignity of the profession. When teachers view both of these norms as being violated by their union, they may wonder about the value of holding these norms and become demoralized.

Furthermore, when teachers believe that their union has yielded too much, they may begin to question the purpose of the union as a body that will uphold the values of the profession and that will protect its members. As Helen mentions, teachers do not stand up for themselves and their profession if they do not see examples of others doing so, especially when they perceive their union as conceding core values.

Holding a job cannot be equated with being a professional. Helen believes that teachers who follow the rules unquestioningly "don't act like professionals in the sense of participating in the dialogue on what's going on or even saying, wait a minute, why do we have to do this?" At their best, Vanessa also believes that unions should enable teachers to make the distinction between following the rules and engaging in morally defensible work. "Unions are important to protect children, and I really don't think people understand that," argued Vanessa. Teachers, in solidarity with their union, could let school leaders know a practice or behavior is harmful to children or the profession without feeling quite as vulnerable individually.

Helen highlighted the sympathetic watchdog role that the Badass Teachers Association has played with the union. She recalled that when the National Education Association took a stand against the outsized role of standardized testing during the reauthorization of the Elementary and Secondary Education Act (ESEA), "the Badass Teachers said, 'Here are the e-mails of the leadership. Send them a note. Tell them thank you.' So I did two block e-mails, one was to the [union] president . . . NEA President Lily Eskelsen [Garcia] e-mailed me back, she said 'Thank you! Keep it up!' and it was so cool."

After teaching for thirty-five years, Helen has renewed faith in her state's union as well. "[The union] has become responsive to teacher dissatisfaction, and they're starting to put forth bills that speak to the problems that are going on." The problems that Helen addressed were not only the bread-and-butter issues about teacher pay and benefits. The union was taking a stand on the well-being of students and the principles that guide good teaching.

However, challenges still remain. In chapter 2, Lee found her building union representatives to be of little help when she was deeply troubled by discriminatory teaching practices in her school. The union building delegates advocated for procedures that undermined equitable student achievement. The union felt like an irrelevant resource for the professional problems she faced.

A VOICE OF PROFESSIONAL CONSCIENCE

Teacher unions could play a much more significant role in conveying the message of professional conscience, or craft conscience, in the words of education philosopher Thomas Green. Not all teachers were as willing to parse their job responsibilities and professional ideals as Jason. Unions could be guides in helping teachers determine when good work and job responsibilities diverge and what course to take in those situations.

Patty, whose experience is detailed in chapter 6, viewed her moral responsibility as fulfilling the expectations as they were outlined by her supervisors or described in policy. As yet, nothing that Patty was asked to do rose to the level of concern for students' well-being. However, Hannah Arendt has shown that the "banality of evil" is fulfilled by civil servants following orders. By generating statements such as "An Ethic for Teachers of Conscience in Public Schools,"[2] the unions could provide teachers with better guidance with what is within the bounds of responsible teaching and what deserves to be questioned.

Unions can improve their messaging to their members, letting them know when they are preserving their power in order to protect not only their members but also the profession itself. Even though the power of unions as labor representation is weakened in some states, as Paul describes what has happened in his state of Wisconsin, unions can continue to establish themselves as a moral force and professional conscience. Examples of this approach can be seen in American Federation of Teachers President Randi Weingarten's weekly advertorials that appear in national news outlets. Targeted messaging of this type at a local level could provide teachers with a common moral vocabulary with which to talk about their profession among themselves, with school leaders, and the broader public.

Teachers often spend a few minutes to several hours a week reading BATs, UOO, and NPE-related posts. These teachers are eager to better understand the policy forces that are shaping their work; they engage in voluntary professional development while they read blogs and participate in synchronous Twitter chats. They form professional learning communities that enable them to interpret their work lives and address the needs of their students. Unions are increasingly using social media to connect their members beyond the boundaries of their schools, districts, and states.

When teachers believe that they have no voice, especially in regards to their daily work, it is possible to become demoralized in addition to disempowered. When teachers become demoralized due to a lack of voice, they may feel isolated by what appears to be a disregard for the moral motivations that drive their work. Teacher unions have an opportunity to elevate individual teachers' voices, which happened with Frank, but also serve as the voice for the profession and public schools. Helen remarked, "The union is our voice, it's our collective voice, it isn't perfect." Unions already possess the power to connect teachers and could use that organizational leverage to stave off demoralization.

LESSONS LEARNED

Teachers want to be proud of being members of a union, but some may need to be convinced that union membership is aligned with the values that attracted them to the profession. Inducting new members into the union will require tapping into the motivations that bring them to teaching.

Union leaders and organizers may consider the following:

- While any organization requires a degree of procedure-based conversation about rights and regulations, limit those to communication that can be accomplished in writing or over e-mail.

- Educate members and the social-justice-oriented left about the history and significance of teacher unions.
- Establish building-level teaching and learning environment climate surveys. After results are in, ask teachers to identify action items and assist in developing an action plan.
- Harness rank-and-file energy. Jason's initial involvement with the union began due to his dissatisfaction with it.
- Provide clear guidance for teachers navigating education law and their professional ethics (e.g., What will happen if a teacher refuses to administer a high-stakes test or informs students of their right to opt out? What are state protections for whistleblowing?).
- Develop messages that are craft-based, rooted in advocating for and protecting the good work teachers are doing.
- Use union platforms to amplify individual teachers' voices in local, state, and national media.
- Offer guidance on teachers' rights regarding the use of social media for professional purposes.
- Connect like-minded activists at different schools, in various districts.
- Raise funds to support hybrid teacher roles that enable a reduced teaching schedule.
- Create member-based inquiry teams to research teachers' concerns and have them publish or present their findings to their peers, leaders, and the media.
- Develop messaging and share resources about the contributions of unions and union members in improving teaching and learning conditions for all in public education.
- Remind members that most teacher assessments include advocacy as a form of ethical behavior so that they can cite this as their reason for speaking up.
- Call on retired union members to publicly voice concerns of professional conscience.

CHAPTER EIGHT

HARNESSING THE POWER
OF RE-MORALIZATION

It was a glorious June day in Maine. After I had traveled the United States interviewing teachers, now the teachers were coming to my workplace for what I called a re-moralization retreat. One of my colleagues joked that it sounded as though I was hosting a religious revival. My goal for the weekend was more modest. Nine of the teachers I interviewed were able to attend, and four additional experienced teachers joined the group for the weekend. I wanted to learn if the concepts I developed for this book resonated with them and to see if we could put some of the re-moralization strategies into practice.

On the doorstep of a house on the Bowdoin College campus, I welcomed teachers with whom I had spoken for about ninety minutes but who now felt like friends. I had been living with their words for months. Although reuniting with the teachers reminded me of details that I had forgotten, I was able to quickly put names and stories to faces.

A woman I didn't recognize approached. I started mentally running through the list of invitees and wondered if I had made a mistake. Did I invite someone with whom I had an initial phone conversation but did not decide to interview? Had the intervening months resulted in my misconnecting words with the memory of a face? No, I determined I had not met this woman before.

She strode toward me with confidence and a buoyant energy, and clearly recognized me. That was a relief. Nonetheless, during our embrace, she sensed my unease. She leaned away, beaming, but still grasping my shoulders, "Doris, it's Carla!"

When I last saw Carla, she looked fifteen years older and, I know now, was eighty pounds heavier. But it was not only her physical appearance that had been transformed. Carla had looked defeated when we spoke eighteen months earlier. She cried multiple times during our conversation. I walked away from the interview wondering if talking with me had caused her more harm than good.

Even after Carla confirmed her identity, I struggled to reconcile this vibrant person, who was easy to laugh and invited others to go out for a jog, with the woman I had interviewed. Prior to the retreat, I would have characterized Carla as the most demoralized teacher I interviewed. Still fiercely committed to doing a good job, she regularly put in twelve- to fourteen-hour days. She found no joy in her work. She had been written up by her principal, who had suggested that she look for another job.

The transformation involved Carla's teaching as well as her physical appearance. After I had bit of time to take in Carla's metamorphosis, I shared my earlier internal monologue and asked, "How did the Carla I met a year and a half ago become the Carla I'm encountering now?" Carla grinned and informed me that this year the very same principal who suggested she should transfer to another school presented her with the building's teacher of the year award. Here's what she told me.

After several years that involved personal and professional challenges, Carla reassessed her life at work and at home. She attempted unsuccessfully to transfer to another district school. Realizing that she would remain at her current school, Carla took a number of strategic actions related to her teaching. First, she put some distance between herself and a dysfunctional grade-level team that was "sucking any joy, hope, and energy out of me." She made a concerted effort to address what had been a clear indication of her demoralization: the principal's censure of Carla's disrespect for her students. Instead, she became mindful of how she responded to students, even when their behavior was out of control. She mentioned that a professional development series on trauma was instrumental in helping her understand the challenges her students were facing. She realized that she must take care of herself in order to be the teacher her students needed. Carla used the summer to recharge and reset her nutrition and fitness regimen.

The principal took notice. Whether by her school leader's design or as a stroke of good luck, Carla's grade-level team membership changed, and now she has collegial support. She has regained the ability to feel as though she is doing good work. The truth is that Carla is still counting down the years until retirement (five and a half), but she says, "My tanks are full and I'm ready for the challenges."

TRANSFORMATION AT ANY ST(AGE)

Through my experience interviewing teachers with moral concerns about their work, I have learned the following lessons:

1. Burnout is not inevitable for experienced teachers.
2. Demoralization may be misdiagnosed as burnout.
3. The remedies for demoralization are not the same as those for burnout.

Carla's transformation, as well as DeeDee's, confirms that it is possible to resuscitate the moral rewards of teaching and revive good work. Both Carla and DeeDee had become teachers who had lost the ability to teach in ways that aligned with their professional commitments and values. They had resigned themselves to going through the motions until retirement. This realization led to their feeling shameful, resentful, and isolated.

Demoralization occurs when teachers can no longer engage in what they consider good work. Carla was overwhelmed by her students' challenging behaviors and her inability to meet their needs. Earlier in her career, Carla had drawn strength from collective action with her colleagues. When the school district had cut funding for specials, she and her grade-level team members established a rotation schedule to ensure that students could still access art, music, and physical education. The last few years had been marked by toxic colleagues who left her unsupported when she faced difficulties developing a healthy learning environment in her classroom. Carla was devastated because she believed the principal's letter of reprimand was an accurate assessment of her behavior. She knew that students needed her respect and love, and that it was her mission to teach and support them even though she was not currently fulfilling her mission.

DeeDee also lost her connection to what made her work good. An expert in math pedagogy who cares deeply about her colleagues, she silenced her concerns about the math textbook they preferred. Then, in the spirit of teamwork, DeeDee followed the textbook to the letter, even though she lamented her own and her students' lack of engagement in the subject. Her students used to say that math was their favorite subject, but no more. For DeeDee, teaching out of the textbook was torture. She knew there was a better way to harness students' enthusiasm for learning and to develop their understanding of mathematical concepts, but she felt she had no choice because the curriculum had been set.

Resorting to conventional accounts of burnout would mischaracterize Carla's and DeeDee's problems. Each teacher possessed clear norms about what students need and deserve. They had well-developed understandings of what it means to be a responsible member of the teaching profession. A great deal of their unhappiness involved the distance between their actions and their beliefs. Carla and DeeDee were not devoid of energy, interest, or expertise. Paradoxically, as with many of the teachers I've interviewed, their deep dissatisfaction with the trajectory of their careers could be attributed to their commitment to the teaching profession and its ideals.

Popular accounts of burnout often depict inexperienced or midcareer teachers who care too much but who fail to conserve their personal resources. They give too much, too soon, and then run out of gas. Carla and DeeDee had already taught for over twenty years when they began to experience deep dissatisfaction with their work. Although it is likely that physical energy will flag as teachers age, waning enthusiasm and energy for the profession are not preordained.

The narrative of teacher burnout depicts the problem as personal and internal to the individual. Teachers, in this account, begin their careers with limited resources that are apportioned in distinct amounts and conserved to varying degrees. One teacher may receive an abundance of resources and use them up quickly, whereas another teacher with fewer resources portions them out slowly, over a longer period of time. According to the burnout narrative, when those individual resources are spent, whether quickly or slowly, a teacher's career ends or sputters along until resignation, retirement, or dismissal.

The ways in which personal resources in teaching are characterized through the burnout narrative are problematic for a number of reasons. The burnout explanation presumes that the resources needed for a career are readily available within each teacher and are apportioned at the beginning of a career. In this account, individuals are solely responsible for managing the resources that have been bestowed by luck (in the case of abundance) or misfortune (in the case of scarcity). In this account, individual teachers are solely responsible for conserving or squandering their limited resources.

The diagnosis of burnout renders the possibility of generating new or renewable resources unlikely. This perspective contributes to ageism. The more experience teachers possess, the more likely they are facing a diminishing shelf life. Like a candle that burns quickly or slowly, the understanding is that so long as it burns, illumination's end is imminent. Ageism in teaching is connected to its feminized status. The feminized status of teaching affects how we see the value of teachers themselves. This is influenced by US cultural assumptions about the value of women as they age and the expertise needed for the work. This reading of teaching helps explain why programs promoting young, inexperienced, and temporary workers are viewed with enthusiasm. Those working in masculinized professions, such as business, law, and medicine, are often valued for the wisdom that accompanies experience and older age.

Moral rewards are the renewable resources that teachers can access when doing good work. To review, individuals engage in good work when they believe (1) the work serves a social purpose that contributes to the well-being of others *and* (2) the way the work is conducted is aligned with that social purpose.[1] Morally motivated teachers engaged in good work can, as Carla explained, "fill their tanks" at any point in their careers. Good work does not need to become less good over time. Teachers can forge meaningful relationships with students year after year. Teachers can develop lessons that help students make sense of their most pressing questions, even as those questions change. Teachers can develop environments that cultivate respect for others and for learning, and those environments shift as students and teachers themselves change.

DEMORALIZATION AND RE-MORALIZATION IN CONTEXT

The renewable resources of moral rewards are found in *doing* good work; they are not discovered as the necessarily limited personal possessions of individual teachers. Therefore, good work depends on the conditions of teaching, not just an individual teacher's motivations, skill, and expertise. The context of teaching provides the backdrop for the action needed to generate the moral rewards. When the context prevents teachers from generating those rewards, demoralization is possible.

Contexts for all kinds of work inevitably change. When shifts occur, teachers and their allies need to develop strategies to ensure that good work can continue. These situations may call for resisting challenges to good work, building new alliances to sustain good work, and revisiting understandings of what it means to do good work. This is the moral work of authentic professional community and the basis for professional ethics.

The approaches that once enabled teachers to access what is good about their work may no longer be effective under the current conditions in which they work. Sometimes teachers will need to readjust their practice to be able to tap into the renewable resources available in good work. Sometimes teachers will need to join together to challenge factors that block their ability to engage in good work. At times, teachers will need to come together to remind themselves of what good work entails.

The profiles of teachers in this book reveal that educators do not need to arrive at a consensus about the methods of good work. In fact, morally engaged teachers may become embroiled in heated disagreements with other morally engaged teachers. Some teachers, like Nina, will focus on the developmental needs of their students. Others, like Edwin, will focus on issues of professional integrity and fairness. What the teachers with a moral sense about their work share is a recognition that their work involves responsibilities to their students and responsibilities to their profession. The particular content and emphasis of these responsibilities may be unique to each teacher but should be recognizable and defensible to others.

For Carla and DeeDee, teaching had once been an outlet to engage in good work. Then it became the source of shame. While experiencing demoralization, neither teacher believed she was contributing to the well-being of students or the integrity of the profession. For Carla, the context of her professional community became toxic and her students' needs intensified. For DeeDee, her pedagogy and curriculum became a straightjacket that filled her with regret. Their work environments created obstacles to accessing the moral rewards of teaching they once enjoyed.

However, in considering their re-moralization, more happened for these experienced teachers than just an internal and personal shift in attitude. They were able to reestablish good work that aligned with their moral motivations because the contexts in which they taught also shifted. Some of the changes came about as a result of their actions and some because of the responsiveness of others (school leaders, colleagues, etc.).

When Carla's principal held her accountable for failing to treat her students with respect, she was devastated. She knew the reprimand to be accurate and justified. Reconnecting with her moral motivations enabled Carla to recalibrate her work and home life. She made a decision to pull away from destructive influences of her colleagues. She then had created enough space to be mindful in her responses to troubling student behaviors, take in what the trauma workshop offered, and develop productive and supportive relationships with a new grade-level team.

DeeDee taught a discovery-based math curriculum during one period she had carved out of the weekly schedule. Yet, this period was insufficient to counteract the damage she felt she was doing by continuing to teach math out of the textbook. Students deserved the best possible instruction, and she was not making it available to them. Fortuitously, DeeDee opened her classroom to a math consultant who was conducting research at the school. At the urging of the consultant, DeeDee approached her new principal to discuss her dissatisfaction with the math curriculum. The principal encouraged DeeDee to abandon the textbook and pursue math instruction guided by her deep pedagogical expertise.

Demoralization occurs as a result of a number of factors that impinge on teachers' ability to do good work. These factors may be changes in policy, curriculum, and personnel. Therefore, re-moralization involves addressing those changes in relation to one's vision of good work, not just changing one's attitude or perspective. Carla and DeeDee proved capable of growing and changing as veteran teachers; they were guided by their professional commitments to do good work in fortuitously responsive contexts. Unlike accounts of burnout that suggest that resources lost are often gone forever, teachers can realign their practices with professional values if they are given the opportunity and support.

WHY DISTINGUISHING BETWEEN BURNOUT AND DEMORALIZATION MATTERS

Teachers may feel affronted and misrecognized by explanations of teacher dissatisfaction and attrition that rely on the concept of burnout. Burnout rests on the assumption that something is wrong with the individual teacher that prevents him or her from succeeding in the job. In demoralization, experienced educators understand that they are facing a conflict between their vision of good work and their teaching context.

Teacher educator and researcher Mary Kennedy has warned educational researchers about what social psychologists call a fundamental attribution error:

> [W]e have veered too far toward the attribution of teaching quality to the characteristics of teachers themselves, and are overlooking situational factors that may have a strong bearing on the quality of the teaching practices we see . . . It is time to look beyond the teacher to the teaching situation itself.[2]

An op-ed in the *New York Times* reveals how medicine is shifting away from the individual blame-game, too. Most discussions of disproportionally high rates of hypertension in the US black population focus on individual lifestyle and personal choices. However, the cardiologist authoring the article asks: what if high blood pressure is the body's reasonable response to the environment for black Americans?[3]

The diagnosis of demoralization does not absolve teachers from any responsibility for their current condition. All the strategies for re-moralization involve teachers taking some form of action. The difference is that the action is not all an "inside job" and may require that they alter their contexts or find alternative outlets for good work. I suspect that teachers experiencing demoralization will be in enough pain to be motivated to take some form of action. Recall that those facing demoralization still want to do good work through teaching but find that they are prevented from doing so. Removing or finding ways around those obstacles is a relief.

Over the course of my decade of research on teachers' moral concerns about their work, I have noticed the rhetorical refrain of the painful loss or disappearance of one's profession, usually through metaphors of death, divorce, or abusive relationships. These feelings were illustrated by the teachers who participated in the retreat. In teams, I asked them to draw how demoralization felt.

The images ranged from trying to extinguish a volcano with a garden hose (hopelessness, impotence), learning that a loved one has a terminal illness (grief, mourning, powerlessness), crawling while concealed by a dark cloud as others looked on from the distance (isolation, shame, self-indictment), being burned alive by relentless requirements and initiatives (overwhelmed, punished), shouting with a megaphone and separated from school leaders and policy makers by a soundproof wall (voiceless, impotent, hopeless), and the familiar images of Sisyphus endlessly trying to push a boulder up a mountain, only to see it roll back (futility, despair, sapping of energy and strength).

The retreat participants and the interviewees experiencing demoralization explained that these feelings were manifested physically as well as emotionally. Teachers experienced feelings of nausea, drowning, and suffocating; felt a need to take flight or disappear; had gastrointestinal problems; were diagnosed with clinical depression; and gained weight. They missed school days, even after having years of perfect attendance. Demoralization has consequences for teacher well-being that may lead to chronic absenteeism as well as attrition.

I later asked participants to provide the definition of demoralization that they took away from the retreat. They understood demoralization as a professional problem as opposed to burnout, which indicates that they have personal issues that impair their professionalism. They remarked that their professional concerns disrupt both their personal and professional lives—meaning the negative impact of demoralization is widespread. The sense of powerlessness to protect the profession they love felt devastating and overwhelming.

Here are some of the definitions provided by the retreat attendees:

Before the retreat, I thought [demoralization] was a combination of people being personally and professionally depressed. I would now consider it strictly a professional life "cause" though the effects certainly can bleed over into someone's personal life. I consider demoralization a teacher's way [of indicating that] the profession has not been what he or she thought it would be or should be. I think it can wax and wane. It can make you leave or make you take no joy in your work or make you a bitter and depressed person even outside of your work.

Demoralization is extreme discouragement bordering on despair that affects teaching, learning, and professionalism. It is brought on by a feeling of helplessness in the face of top-down or bureaucratic systems that seem resistant to change.

Demoralization is losing sight of the thing(s) that inspired you to teach in the first place and then falling in line with the "system" as it exists. Demoralization is when you have lost your passion for the job and it is just a job, but it was the job requirements that "others" created that did it to you and not the job itself. Demoralization means that given the right mix of circumstances (admin, coworkers, funding, etc.) you could re-moralize and thrive. Demoralization means that it was stolen from you, not willingly given up. There is a light and a hope, but it gets further away the more it is not addressed.

When teachers have a conscious or unconscious dissatisfaction that they did not previously have with the teaching profession, due to ethical/moral conflicts from corporate education reform and the attack on public education.

Not feeling "good" about what I am doing.

The distinction between demoralization and burnout was also important for the teachers who attended the retreat. The difference enabled them to reframe themselves as agents who continue to strive to do good work. While the distinction does not automatically alter the challenging contexts in which many of them teach, naming the experience of demoralization enabled them to better identify the obstacles to good work. The professional community that we generated reduced their feelings of shame and isolation, replacing them with a sense of solidarity and possibility.

I think using two different words is so important. Because burnout is some kind of personal deficiency . . . but demoralization is definitely imposed on good teachers by outside corrupt or misguided forces. And demoralization needs to be treated by addressing the disease (those forces) rather than the symptoms (the teacher's negative experiences).

Helping understand the difference between demoralization and burnout has helped me immensely mentally. It has allowed me to reflect on the harder times of teaching and reaffirm that I'm not tired of teaching, I'm tired with the BS that I have to fight while simultaneously teaching.

I think the way you described it—watching a loved one die [demoralization] versus being sick yourself [burnout]—is perfect. Because there is this sense that you have little control over what is happening, and you'll have to live afterwards. If you stay or leave, you still have the good and bad memories, and what you loved has basically been taken from you. And to further the disease metaphor, there are people and foundations who have intentionally given this disease to your loved one. So that makes it even worse.

Because burnout implies being tired and just needing a break. Burnout also implies that the fault lies within. Demoralization implies that the fault lies with the exterior and outside changes we feel when we have no control over. Burnout can possibly be fixed [more easily than demoralization] with time off and self-care. Demoralization is much more difficult to fix and the repercussions are more pervasive.

If you can label it and talk about it, you can better address it and face it. Burnout is such a huge, nameless, faceless blob of a problem that it seems all-consuming . . . but re-moralization feels like it can be targeted and confronted. To "re" anything is to remind yourself of why you do what you do and for whom—it feels like there is an "again" coming. Burnout means the fuel/wick is spent and there is nothing more to give. When there is nothing more to give, there is no more hope, motivation, or struggle for self. YOU burn out, but it feels like re-moralization comes from other places, which means it can be addressed.

Burnout comes from within each person. Perhaps a teacher wants to retire but needs a few more years and is just putting in the time. If students and colleagues sense this, it is often written off as burnout. Demoralization comes from society and is like a million tiny spears puncturing a teacher who loves his/her job and feels it is an important and ethical career. As the media promotes the lies of corporate ed reform and the public internalizes those messages as truths, students, families, and community members who once trusted and respected us no longer do. There is no evidence in the ed reform lies, and because people believe what they hear without questioning it, teachers become defenders of themselves and their practice instead of respected professionals. The deprofessionalization of the teaching profession is demoralizing and is totally different from burnout.

Demoralization can be fixed.

With a better diagnosis, teachers with moral concerns about their work can have less dis-ease. They come to recognize the worthiness of their pursuit of good work in a professional community composed of others who also bring moral commitments and values to teaching. These specific values do not need to be identical, but the recognition of a shared commitment to good work provides the basis for many of the strategies that may promote re-moralization.

PROFESSIONAL ETHICS IN PRACTICE

These are demoralizing times for many teachers. Gardner, Csikszentmihalyi, and Damon explain that what they call difficult times "expose the threats to good work and may mobilize people to struggle productively, to confirm the essence of their calling, embrace high standards, and reaffirm their personal identities."[4] The upside of demoralization is that it indicates a situation or context that needs to be changed or altered. When teachers work together to alter the situations that need to be changed, they begin to reverse the process of demoralization and build professional community.

When teachers engage in conversations about the challenges of enacting their professional commitments in relation to the conditions of teaching, they are engaged in professional ethics. In those conversations, they are making public the values they bring to their work. They are making public what enables or prevents them from cultivating good work. If teaching conditions present ongoing and persistent challenges to good work, teachers need to ask: Can I fulfill this responsibility in a new way? If not, is this a value that is worth fighting for? What would need to change in order to be able to enact this value? Can I continue to work with my moral center being compromised in this way?

Teachers who cannot find ways to resolve the value conflicts that they encounter in their work may leave as conscientious objectors to teaching.[5] They will leave teaching rather than seriously compromise their professional commitments. School leaders, unions, and colleagues can intervene before teachers resign as conscientious objectors and prior to experiencing demoralization.

Nearly all the teachers I have met explained that they have had few opportunities to articulate their understanding of good work. Those who did often used their individual voice, through blogging or letters to the editor, to speak to a wider audience. Few of these teachers, absent those who had engaged in activist activities, had articulated their vision of good work in conversation with other teachers. Nearly all the teachers remarked that they have no structured opportunities to reflect on how school policies and practices affect their ability to engage in good work.

Engaging in conversations about good teaching and good work is different from determining who is and is not a good teacher. Educational researchers, like myself, can leverage our status and access to publishing and speaking outlets to amplify teachers' voices. We need narratives, not of heroes who persevere through impossible demands, but of teachers who weigh how they can do good work in the face of everyday requirements that might subvert their professional commitments. We need to listen to the moral claims that experienced teachers make when they criticize their work conditions, policies, and practices. We need to hear teachers' claims as moral commentary on a moral profession. Their collective voices are persuasive and give us insight into the status of the project of public education in the United States.

Professional ethics take place through deliberation and conversation. At times, professional ethics will entail questions about what is the right course of action in a particular situation. Other times, conversations about professional ethics will entail asking the broader questions about what it means to participate in and enact good work.

When engaging in conversations about what good work entails with individuals outside the profession, teachers need to be prepared that the conversation may be assumed to be self-interested. Teachers can be better prepared to hold their ground by naming their moral concerns as moral and refusing the attribution that their concerns are personal preferences.

After fifteen years of experience, Reggie knows where he stands as a teacher. He is confident in his abilities and unwavering in his dedication to the work. With two master's degrees, he serves as visiting faculty in prestigious universities nearby. He is well compensated—at the top of the pay scale in his district, which has the highest salaries in the state. Nonetheless, he was looking for a way out and was applying for doctoral programs in urban education.

Reggie is passionate about teaching. His accounts of his first year were enough to convince his girlfriend to enroll in a teacher education program and enter the profession. He has threatened me that he could tell me stories about teaching all night. He is enamored of the diverse and challenging community where he works, describing it as "magical." His goal is to "do the right thing by kids."

Difficult times have become the norm. Reggie had seventeen administrators come and go in the last ten years. He witnessed the entire faculty in a nearby school receive pink slips. Even though all the staff ultimately were extended new offers at the same school, the strongest teachers had already accepted other positions. He watched his teaching environment move from a place where he was highly valued for his innovative approaches to engaging students in literature to a "top-down, fill-in-the bubble" context.

With extensive background in linking literacy and the arts, Reggie's classroom used to be a hum of activity. Students would be updating a Japanese folktale, turning a Shakespeare sonnet into a play, cutting up an Emily Dickinson poem to make a new text. He saw his role as designing these engaging and purposeful learning opportunities so that he could then support students through critique and encouragement. Ongoing collaborative projects enabled students to develop the skills of self-monitoring and team building.

Now, Reggie monitors a classroom where students click through an online literacy program that supplies student data directly to the district. His experience, he believes, "is endemic of a cultural shift to teacher as worker rather than teacher as professional. Teacher as the deliverer . . . the curriculum delivery machine." He believes that this shift has allowed programs like Teach For America to proliferate, and that is demoralizing. "It galls me that with six weeks of training, you are allowed entrance into this profession to which I have devoted my entire career, significant amounts of money, and education, and training, and practice."

For a person like Reggie, finding nowhere to place his intellectual energy in teaching has become disorienting and depressing. "The expertise that I may have and bring is no longer really wanted," he explained. The desire to be valued as an intellectual attracts Reggie to higher education. His affiliations with local universities have been his lifeline. Ending his work at the school and then working at the teacher education program "is night and day. Suddenly, I'm in a place where people value what I have to say and I feel productive. And smart!"

When working with student teachers, Reggie stresses that they find allies and be able to provide pedagogical justification for everything they do. When you are a break-the-mold teacher, he recommends, you want to be able to provide a clear rationale and purpose for each and every move. Reggie is passing along what he sees as the core of professional *integrity. It is necessary to provide reasons and to hold the line when needed.*

"My teacher education program gave me the intellectual vocabulary to say 'no.'"

Reggie, like so many teachers I spoke to for this book, entered teaching because it was an intellectually vibrant way to do good work. Over the course of his career, he has found it increasingly difficult to live the professional values that sustained him for many years. The intellectual dimensions of his work disappeared.

Educators who experience demoralization are not saying "no" to the teaching profession. They are struggling to enact good work in a pedagogical policy environment that is often deaf to their moral concerns. When teachers cannot uphold professional values and commitments, when they cannot access the moral rewards of their work, they become demoralized.

These are demoralizing times for public school teachers, but they need not be defeatist times. Experienced teachers, and retired teachers as well, can recognize their collective power to shine a light on the ways that students are not being well served, and when appropriate, when young people in public schools are being harmed. Collectively, teachers can point to ways that the profession is being degraded. Difficult and demoralizing times issue a challenge to a profession. They inspire practitioners to declare what they stand for.

WAYS TO ATTENUATE TEACHER ATTRITION

Effectively remedying teacher attrition is impossible if we are examining only a portion of the problem of teacher dissatisfaction. Educational researchers need to refine their inquiries so they may capture the moral dimensions of teacher attrition. When teachers bring moral motivations to their work, it is possible that moral concerns could cause them to leave.

The US Department of Education School Staffing Survey and the Teacher Follow-up Survey do not include items that enable teachers to signal moral concerns about their work. Additional items that could capture these types of concerns could be: Do you believe that you are able to teach in ways that serve students well? Do you believe that fulfilling your job responsibilities has harmed your students? Your profession? There may be concern that teachers' responses could criticize and undermine federal and state policies. However, the current teacher shortage may provide sufficient rationale to gather as much data as possible to stave off teacher attrition.

Heather Carlson-Jacquez has developed an instrument to measure teacher demoralization.[6] School leaders and unions could use this survey to assess the degree and type of moral concerns among teachers. A more finely tuned tool such as this reveals both the kinds of moral commitments that teachers bring to their work and the ways that they are unable to enact them.

Teacher educators, like myself, can help novice teachers develop a vision for good work. This usually takes the form of an articulated "philosophy of teaching." Our role is to enable new teachers to sustain and enact the normative commitments when they are inducted into the profession. In preparation for that transition, we can present teachers with cases that ask them to envision how they might continue to live their values in the face of challenging policies and environments. We can also give teachers the intellectual vocabulary to say "no," when necessary.

Notes

INTRODUCTION

1. Christopher Day and Qi Gu, "Variations in the Conditions for Teachers' Professional Learning and Development: Sustaining Commitment and Effectiveness over a Career," *Oxford Review of Education* 33, no. 4 (2007): 423–43; Caroline F. Mansfield, Susan Beltman, Anne Price, and Andrew McConney, "'Don't Sweat the Small Stuff': Understanding Teacher Resilience at the Chalkface," *Teaching and Teacher Education* 28, no. 3 (2012): 347–67; Janice H. Patterson, Loucrecia Collins, and Gypsy Abbott, "A Study of Teacher Resilience in Urban Schools," *Journal of Instructional Psychology* 31, no. 1 (2004): 3–11.

2. Susan Moore Johnson and The Project on the Next Generation of Teachers, *Finders and Keepers: Helping New Teachers Survive and Thrive in Our Schools* (San Francisco: Jossey-Bass, 2004).

3. Doris A. Santoro with Lisa Morehouse, "Teaching's Conscientious Objectors: Principled Leavers of High-Poverty Schools," *Teachers College Record* 113, no. 12 (2011): 2671–705.

4. One notable limitation of this group of interviewees is the lack of racial diversity. With the dearth of teachers of color entering and remaining in the profession, it is especially important to hear their voices and to learn if moral concerns weigh into their decisions to enter, stay, or leave. Here are some characteristics of the twenty-three experienced teachers who expressed moral concerns about their work, at the time of the interviews in 2014–2015:

   • Seven taught for five to twelve years, six from thirteen to nineteen years, and eight for over twenty years.

- The total teaching experience of the group is 370 years.
- Fourteen taught in urban schools, six in suburban, and two in rural.
- The schools are located in New England, the Mid-Atlantic, the Midwest, and the South.
- Fifteen taught in schools considered high-need. Some have been "turnaround" schools or have been operating under the long-term threat of closure.
- One worked at a school that is internationally recognized and visited for its inquiry-based approach.
- Three of the districts where the teachers taught appear regularly in magazine lists of the US's best schools.
- Eight of the teachers I interviewed worked in elementary schools, four at the middle school/junior high level, and nine in high schools.
- They taught art, English, English language learners, history, library media studies, math, science, special education, and world languages.
- Three had won state- or national-level awards for teaching.
- Two were National Board certified teachers, two were pursuing National Board Teacher Certification.
- Some identify as ardent rule followers, whereas others characterize themselves as renegades.
- All but two, who identify as Latinx, are white.
- Fourteen are women. Nine are men. All are cisgendered.
- Some are in same-sex relationships.

CHAPTER 1

1. Leib Sutcher, Linda Darling-Hammond, and Desiree Carver-Thomas, *A Coming Crisis in Teaching? Teacher Supply, Demand, and Shortages in the U.S.* (Palo Alto, CA: Learning Policy Institute, 2016).
2. Ibid.
3. Ibid.
4. Richard Ingersoll, "Teacher Turnover and Teacher Shortages: An Organizational Analysis," *American Educational Research Journal* 38, no. 3 (2001): 499–534.
5. Sutcher et al., "Coming Crisis," 4.
6. MetLife, *The MetLife Survey of the American Teacher: Challenges for School Leadership* (New York: MetLife, 2013); Office of Performance Evaluations, *Workforce Issues Affecting Public School Teachers* (Boise: Idaho Legislature, 2013).

7. American Federation of Teachers and Badass Teachers Association, *Quality of Worklife Survey* 2015, http://www.aft.org/sites/default/files/worklifesurveyresults2015.pdf.

8. Dave Umhoefer, "For Unions in Wisconsin, a Hard and Fast Fall Since Act 10," *Milwaukee Journal Sentinel*, November 27, 2016, http://projects.jsonline.com/news/2016/11/27/for-unions-in-wisconsin-fast-and-hard-fall-since-act-10.html.

9. Geraldine J. Clifford, *Those Good Gertrudes: A Social History of Women Teachers in America* (Baltimore, MD: Johns Hopkins University Press, 2014).

10. Kristin Buras, "The Mass Termination of Black Veteran Teachers in New Orleans: Cultural Politics, the Education Market, and Its Consequences," *The Educational Forum*, 60, no. 2 (2016): 154–70.

11. Richard M. Ingersoll and David A. Perda, "The Status of Teaching as a Profession," in *Schools and Society: A Sociological Approach to Education*, eds. Jeanne Ballantine and Joan Spade (Los Angeles: Pine Forge Press, 2008), 106–18.

12. Gallup, *The State of America's Schools: The Path to Winning Again in Education,* 2014, http://www.gallup.com/services/178709/state-america-s chools-report.aspx.

13. Ingersoll and Perda, "Status," 117.

14. Pasi Sahlberg, *Finnish Lessons: What Can the World Learn from Educational Change in Finland?* (New York: Teachers College Press, 2014), 99–103; H. Richard Milner, *Policy Reforms and De-Professionalization of Teaching* (Boulder, CO: National Education Policy Center, 2013), http://nepc.colorado.edu/publication/policy-reforms-deprofessionalization.

15. Linda Valli, Robert G. Croninger, Marilyn J. Chambliss, Anno O. Graeber, and Daria Buese, *Test Driven: High-Stakes Accountability in Elementary Schools* (New York: Teachers College Press, 2008), 161.

16. Michael W. Apple and Susan Jungck, "'You Don't Have to Be a Teacher to Teach This Unit:' Teaching, Technology and Gender in the Classroom," *American Educational Research Journal* 27, no. 2 (1990): 227–51.

17. Andy Hargreaves, *Changing Teachers, Changing Times: Teachers' Work and Culture in the Postmodern Age* (London: A&C Black, 2001).

18. Steve Suitts, *A New Majority Research Bulletin: Low Income Students Now a Majority in the Nation's Public Schools* (Atlanta, GA: Southern Education Foundation, 2015), http://www.southerneducation.org/Our-Strategies/Research-and-Publications/New-Majority-Diverse

-Majority-Report-Series/A-New-Majority-2015-Update-Low-Income
-Students-Now.

19. Southern Poverty Law Center, *The Trump Effect: The Impact of the 2016 Presidential Election on Our Nation's Schools,* 2016, https://www.splcenter.org/20161128/trump-effect-impact-2016-presidential-election-our-nations-schools.

20. Anne Podolsky, Tara Kini, Joseph Bishop, and Linda Darling-Hammond, "Sticky Schools: How to Find and Keep Teachers in the Classroom," *Phi Delta Kappan* 98, no. 8 (2017): 19–25.

21. Elizabeth Campbell, "Ethical Intentions and the Moral Motivation of Teachers," in *Handbook of Moral Motivation: Theories, Models, Applications*, eds. Karin Heinrichs, Fritz Oser, and Terence Lovat (The Netherlands: Sense Publishers, 2013), 517–32; David T. Hansen, *The Call to Teach* (New York: Teachers College Press, 1995).

22. Daniel C. Lortie, "The Teacher's Shame: Anger and the Normative Commitments of Classroom Teachers," *The School Review* 75, no. 2 (1967): 155–71.

23. Thomas F. Green, "The Formation of Conscience in an Age of Technology," *American Journal of Education* 94, no. 1 (1985): 1–32.

CHAPTER 2

1. This chapter draws on an argument that I made originally in Doris A. Santoro, "Good Teaching in Difficult Times: Demoralization in the Pursuit of Good Work," *American Journal of Education* 188, no. 1 (2011): 1–23.

2. Howard Gardner, Mihaly Csikszentmihalyi, and William Damon, *Good Work: When Excellence and Ethics Meet* (New York: Basic Books, 2001).

CHAPTER 3

1. Doris A. Santoro with Lisa Morehouse, "Teaching's Conscientious Objectors: Principled Leavers of High-Poverty Schools," *Teachers College Record* 113, no. 12 (2011): 2671–705.

CHAPTER 4

1. Daniel C. Lortie, "The Teacher's Shame: Anger and the Normative Commitments of Classroom Teachers," *The School Review* 75, no. 2 (1967): 155.

2. Doris A. Santoro, "'I Was Becoming Increasingly Uneasy About the Profession and What Was Being Asked of Me': Preserving Integrity in Teaching," *Curriculum Inquiry* 43, no. 5 (2013): 563–87.

3. See Meira Levinson and Jacob Fay, *Dilemmas of Educational Ethics: Cases and Commentaries* (Cambridge, MA: Harvard Education Press, 2016).

4. Doris A. Santoro, "Teachers' Expressions of Craft Conscience: Upholding the Integrity of a Profession," *Teachers and Teaching: Theory and Practice* 23, no. 6 (2017): 750–761.

5. Thomas F. Green, "The Formation of Conscience in an Age of Technology," *American Journal of Education* 94, no. 1 (1985): 23.

6. Alasdair MacIntyre, *After Virtue*, 2nd ed. (Notre Dame, IN: University of Notre Dame, 1984).

CHAPTER 5

1. Christopher Day and Qi Gu, *The New Lives of Teachers* (New York: Routledge, 2010), 156. Christopher Day and Qi Gu, "Variations in the Conditions for Teachers' Professional Learning and Development: Sustaining Commitment and Effectiveness over a Career," *Oxford Review of Education* 33, no. 4 (2007): 423–43; Caroline F. Mansfield, Susan Beltman, Anne Price, and Andrew McConney, "'Don't Sweat the Small Stuff': Understanding Teacher Resilience at the Chalkface," *Teaching and Teacher Education* 28, no. 3 (2012): 347–67; Janice H. Patterson, Loucrecia Collins, and Gypsy Abbott, "A Study of Teacher Resilience in Urban Schools," *Journal of Instructional Psychology* 31, no. 1 (2004): 3–11.

2. Doris A. Santoro, "Teachers' Expressions of Craft Conscience: Upholding the Integrity of a Profession," *Teachers and Teaching: Theory and Practice* 23, no. 6 (2017): 750–761.

3. Christopher Emdin, "The Failure Cycle Causing a Shortage of Black Male Teachers," *PBS Newshour*, January 26, 2017, http://www.pbs.org/newshour/bb/failure-cycle-causing-shortage-black-male-teachers/.

4. Santoro, "Teachers' Expressions"; Doris A. Santoro with Lisa Morehouse, "Teaching's Conscientious Objectors: Principled Leavers of High-Poverty Schools," *Teachers College Record* 113, no. 12 (2011): 2671–705.

CHAPTER 6

1. Leib Sutcher, Linda Darling-Hammond, and Desiree Carver-Thomas, *A Coming Crisis in Teaching? Teacher Supply, Demand, and Shortages in the U.S.* (Palo Alto, CA: Learning Policy Institute, 2016).

2. Matthew A. Kraft, William H. Marinell, and Derrick Shen-Wei Yee, "School Organizational Contexts, Teacher Turnover, and Student

Achievement: Evidence from Panel Data," *American Educational Research Journal* 53, no. 5 (2016): 1411–49.

3. Jim Knight, "What Can We Do About Teacher Resistance?" *Phi Delta Kappan* 90, no. 7 (2009): 508–13; Kathryn B. McKenzie and James J. Scheurich, "Teacher Resistance to Improvement of Schools with Diverse Students," *International Journal of Leadership in Education* 11, no. 2 (2008): 117–33; Ewald Terhart, "Teacher Resistance Against School Reform: Reflecting an Inconvenient Truth," *School Leadership and Management* 33, no. 5 (2013): 486–500. doi.org/10.1080/136324 34.2013.793494.

4. Betty Achinstein and Rodney T. Ogawa, "(In)Fidelity: What the Resistance of New Teachers Reveals About Professional Principles and Prescriptive Educational Policies," *Harvard Educational Review* 76, no. 1 (2006): 30–63, 55.

5. Doris A. Santoro, "'We're Not Going to Do That Because It's Not Right': Using Pedagogical Responsibility to Reframe the Doublespeak of Fidelity," *Educational Theory* 66, no. 1–2 (2016): 263–77.

6. John Hildebrand, "NY Education Commissioner Says Opt-outs 'Not Reasonable,'" *Newsday*, August 20, 2015, http://www.newsday.com /long-island/maryellen-elia-nyeducation-commissioner-says-test-opt -outs-not-reasonable-1.10759569.

7. Doris A. Santoro, "Cassandra in the Classroom: Teaching and Moral Violence," *Studies in Philosophy and Education* 36, no. 1 (2017): 49–60.

CHAPTER 7

1. For a more detailed account of Jason's criticism of the curriculum, see Doris A. Santoro, "'We're Not Going to Do That Because It's Not Right': Using Pedagogical Responsibility to Reframe the Doublespeak of Fidelity," *Educational Theory* 66, no. 1–2 (2016): 263–77.

2. Teachers of Conscience, "An Ethic for Teachers of Conscience in Public Education," https://teachersofconscience.wordpress.com/ethics/.

CHAPTER 8

1. Howard Gardner, Mihaly Csikszentmihalyi, and William Damon, *Good Work: When Excellence and Ethics Meet* (New York: Basic Books, 2001).

2. Mary M. Kennedy, "Attribution Error and the Quest for Teacher Quality," *Educational Researcher* 39, no. 8 (2010): 591.

3. Sandeep Jauhar, "When Blood Pressure Is Political," *New York Times,* August 7, 2016, https://www.nytimes.com/2016/08/07/opinion /sunday/when-blood-pressure-is-political.html.

4. Gardner, Csikszentmihalyi, and Damon, *Good Work,* 6.

5. Doris A. Santoro with Lisa Morehouse, "Teaching's Conscientious Objectors: Principled Leavers of High-Poverty Schools," *Teachers College Record* 113, no. 12 (2011): 2671–705.

6. Heather A. Carlson-Jacquez, "Development of an Instrument to Measure K–12 Teacher Demoralization in a Test-Based Accountability Context" (Unpublished dissertation, Virginia Commonwealth University, 2016), http://scholarscompass.vcu.edu/etd/4541/.

Acknowledgments

Many expressions of gratitude are required for ten years of research:

To all the teachers whose experiences have contributed to this book and beyond, thank you for trusting me with your stories.

To the Bowdoin College students who have supported this research, you have provided an invaluable service: Leah Alper, Elina Berglund, Kate Berkley, Ramaa Chitale, Kaitee Dailey, Sammie Francis, Diego Guerrero, Anna Martens, Sophie Meyers, Roya Moussapour, Mitsuki Nishimoto, Luke Potter, Perla Rubi, Sarah Steffen, Ryan Szantyr, Serena Taj, and Anna Williams.

To my Education Department colleagues past and present, especially Dino Anderson, Katie Byrnes, Chuck Dorn, Nancy Jennings, Casey Meehan, and Alison Miller, thank you for listening to my processing and for harborside working lunches. Special thanks to George Isaacson, who educated me about whistleblower cases. Lynn Brettler made the retreat a success.

To Bowdoin College for indispensable funding.

To David T. Hansen, you provided me with a model for how to integrate philosophical and empirical research.

To Katharine Atwood, you transformed my thoughts into a polished graphic.

To Nancy Walser, you empowered me to write what I know.

To my parents, you made all this possible.

To my finest motivators, Toby and Nat, you encourage me to get my work done efficiently so we can go have adventures together.

About the Author

Doris A. Santoro is an associate professor at Bowdoin College, where she serves as chair of the Education Department. She teaches courses in educational studies and teacher education. Her philosophical and qualitative research examines teachers' moral concerns about their work and their moral arguments for resistance. She has taught high school English in Brooklyn and San Francisco, GED prep at an alternative to incarceration program in Manhattan, and worked as a bilingual literacy consultant in Jersey City.

Index